PURE ANIMAL WISDOM

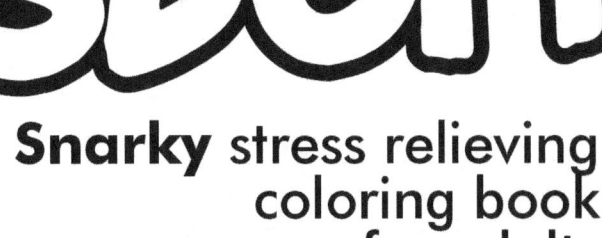

Snarky stress relieving
coloring book
for adults

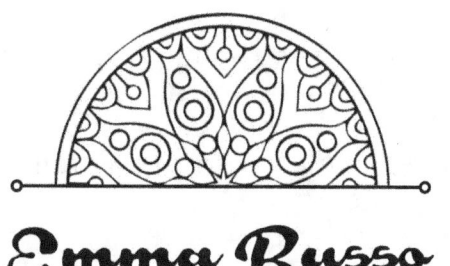

Emma Russo

Introduction

Surrender to the wonderful designs and indulge in the wonder of peace of mind. Release the animal you have inside!

Have you realized that animals are the best Mindfulness teachers? They don't live wondering if they paid the bills or if their partner called, they live in the present and surrender to the wonders of life.

Ready? The good stuff is about to begin! My name is Emma Russo and my passion is creative Mindfulness to unwind yourself from everything, and bringing it to everyone with a little spark, fun and irreverence is my mission in this book.

I truly congratulate you for embracing the art of Mindfulness along with the wildest animals. Mindfulness is an art used for many years to reduce levels of stress, anxiety, insomnia and invites us to wonderful states of relaxation for those who practice it. It is never too late to start practicing, unless you are a bottle of wine or a good cheese, age does not matter!

It is time to relax in your favorite place, leaving everything and everyone aside. This just begins! With this book you will be able to calm your emotions as if calming a wild colt, or maybe…. you will unleash the wild colt that you have inside!

I wish you every success in this new adventure.

Emma R.

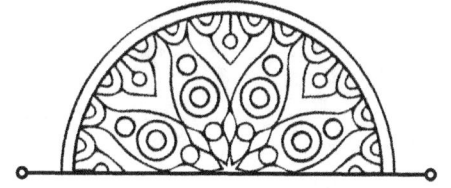

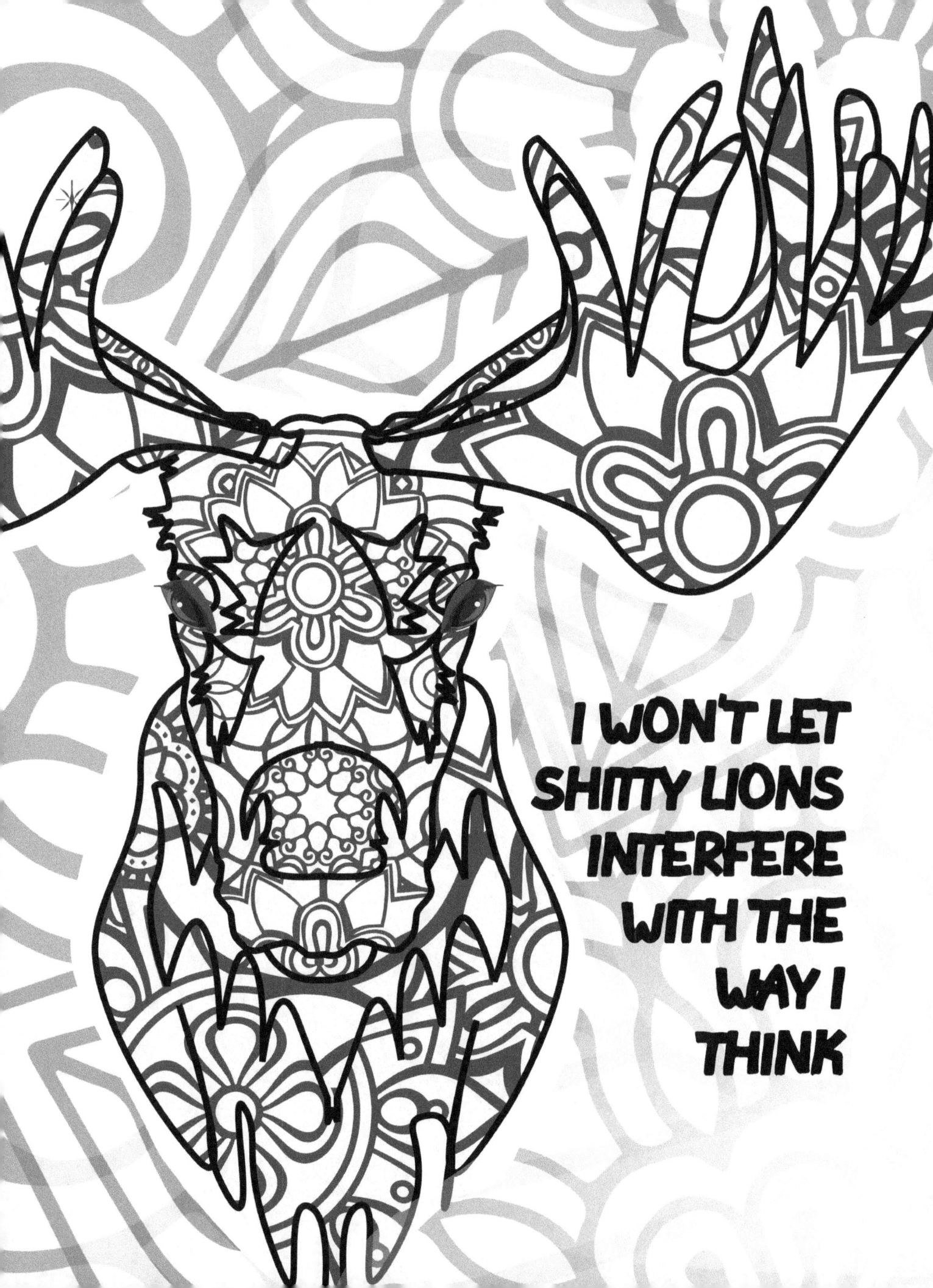

THERE ARE THINGS YOU ALWAYS END UP SEEING, THE SUN, THE MOON AND THE F*CKING TRUTH

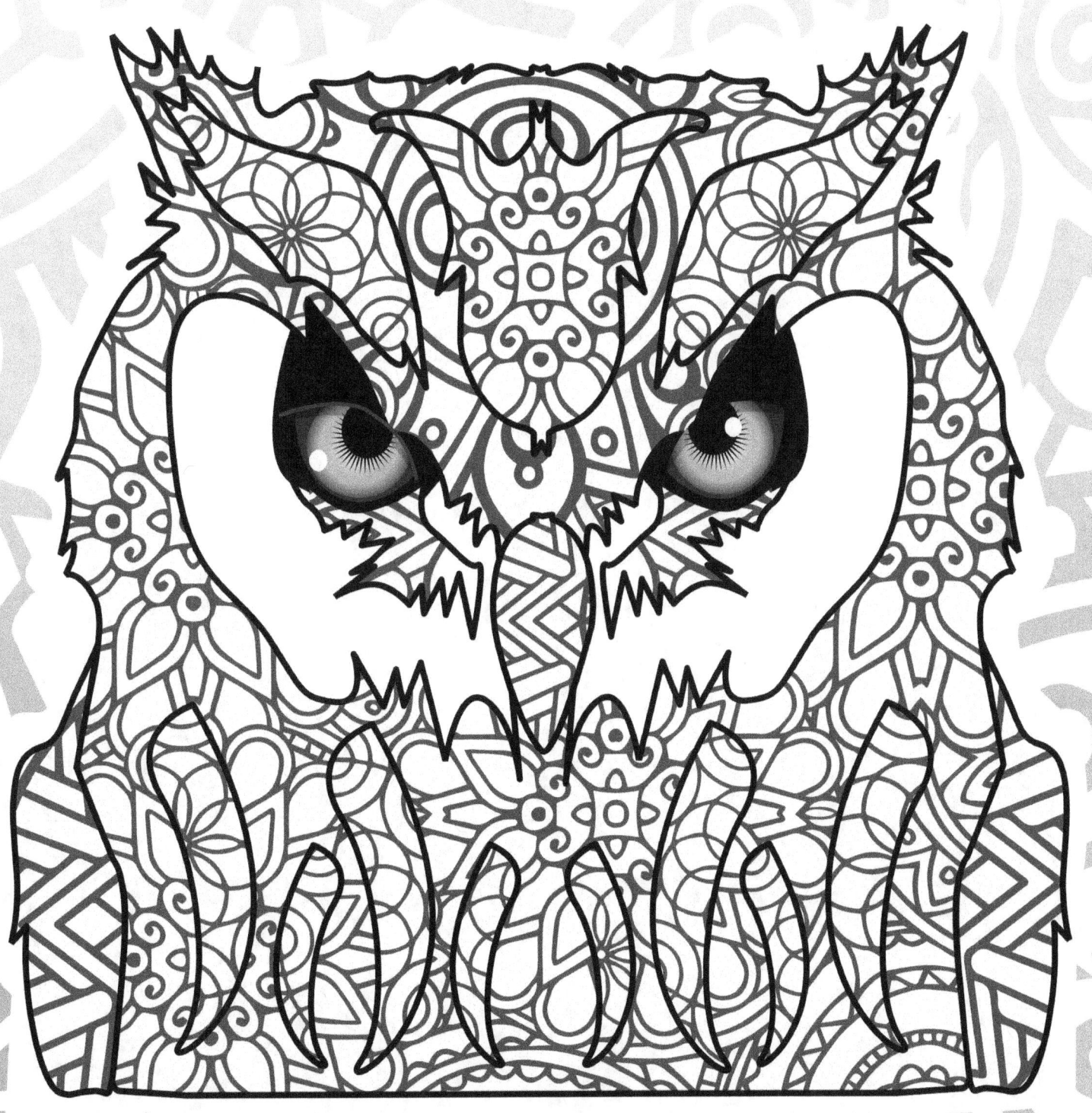

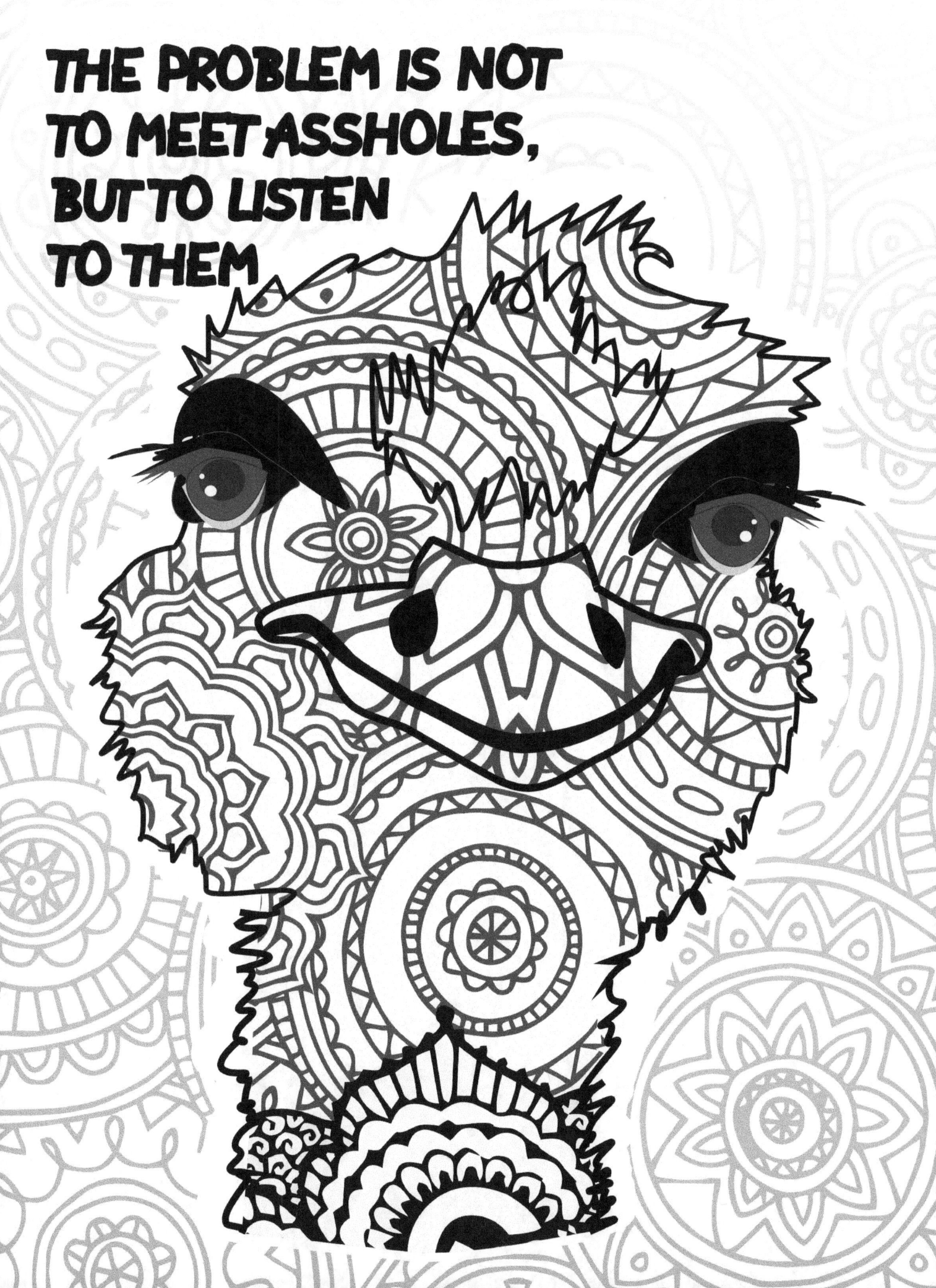

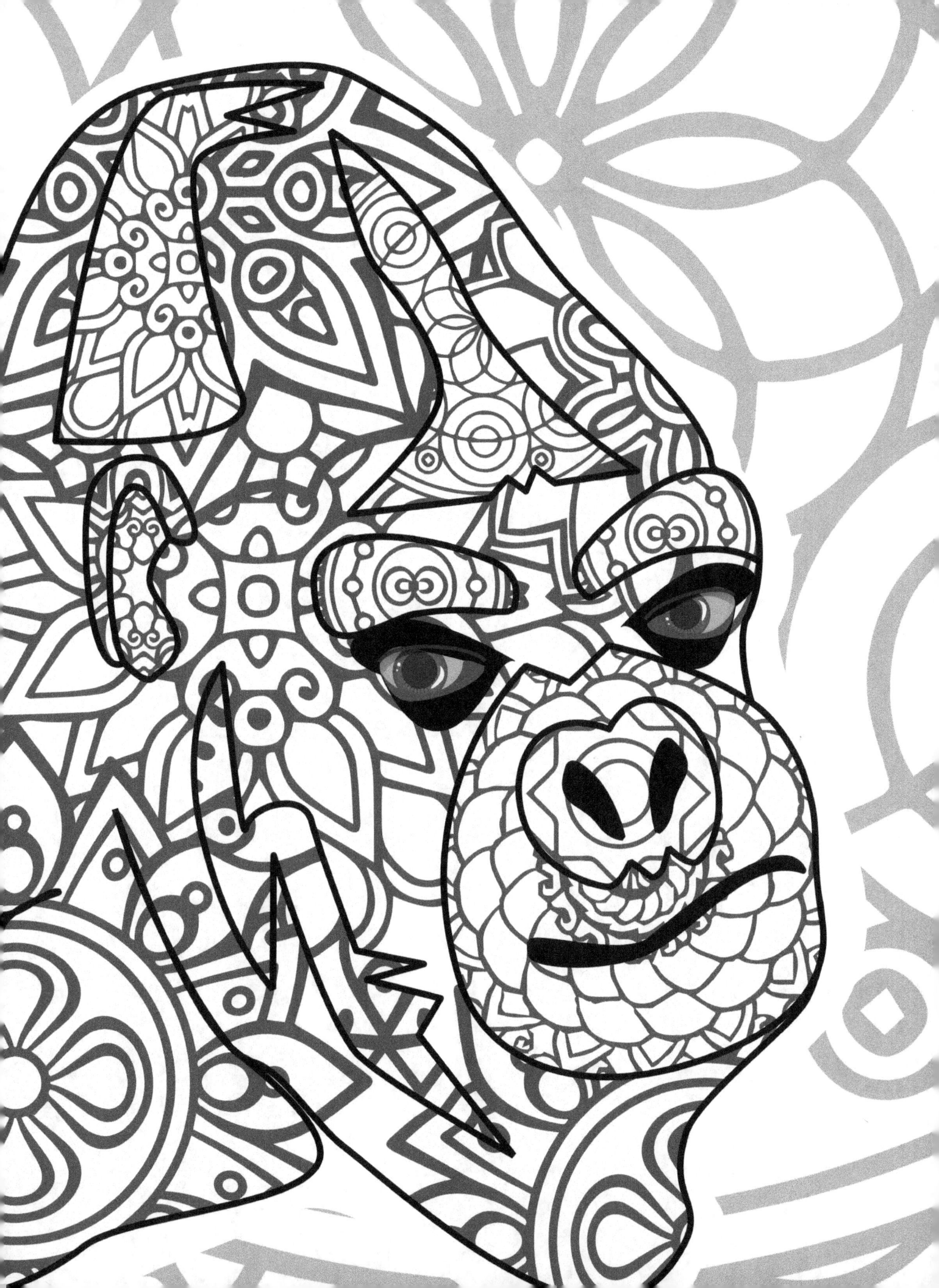

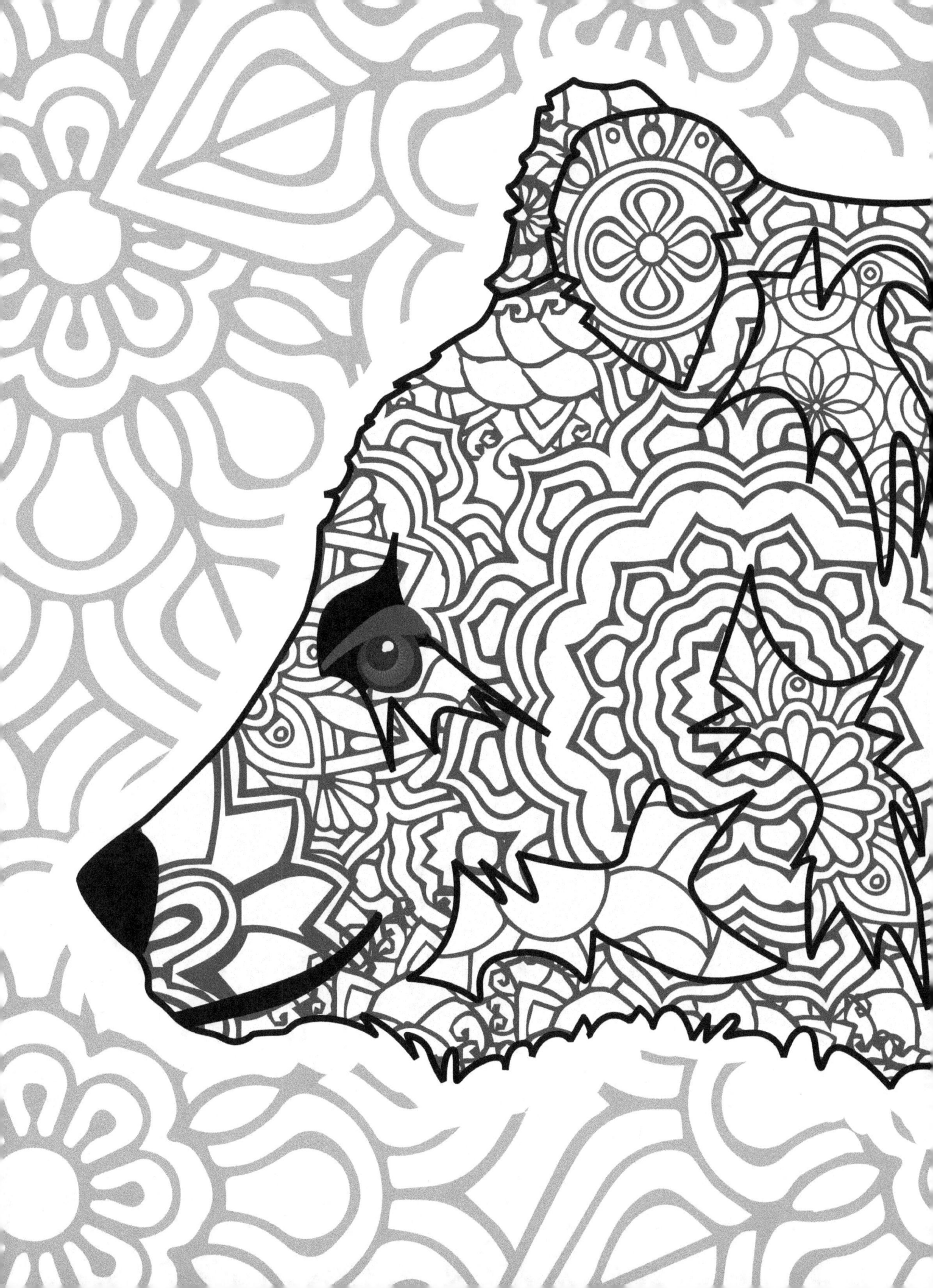

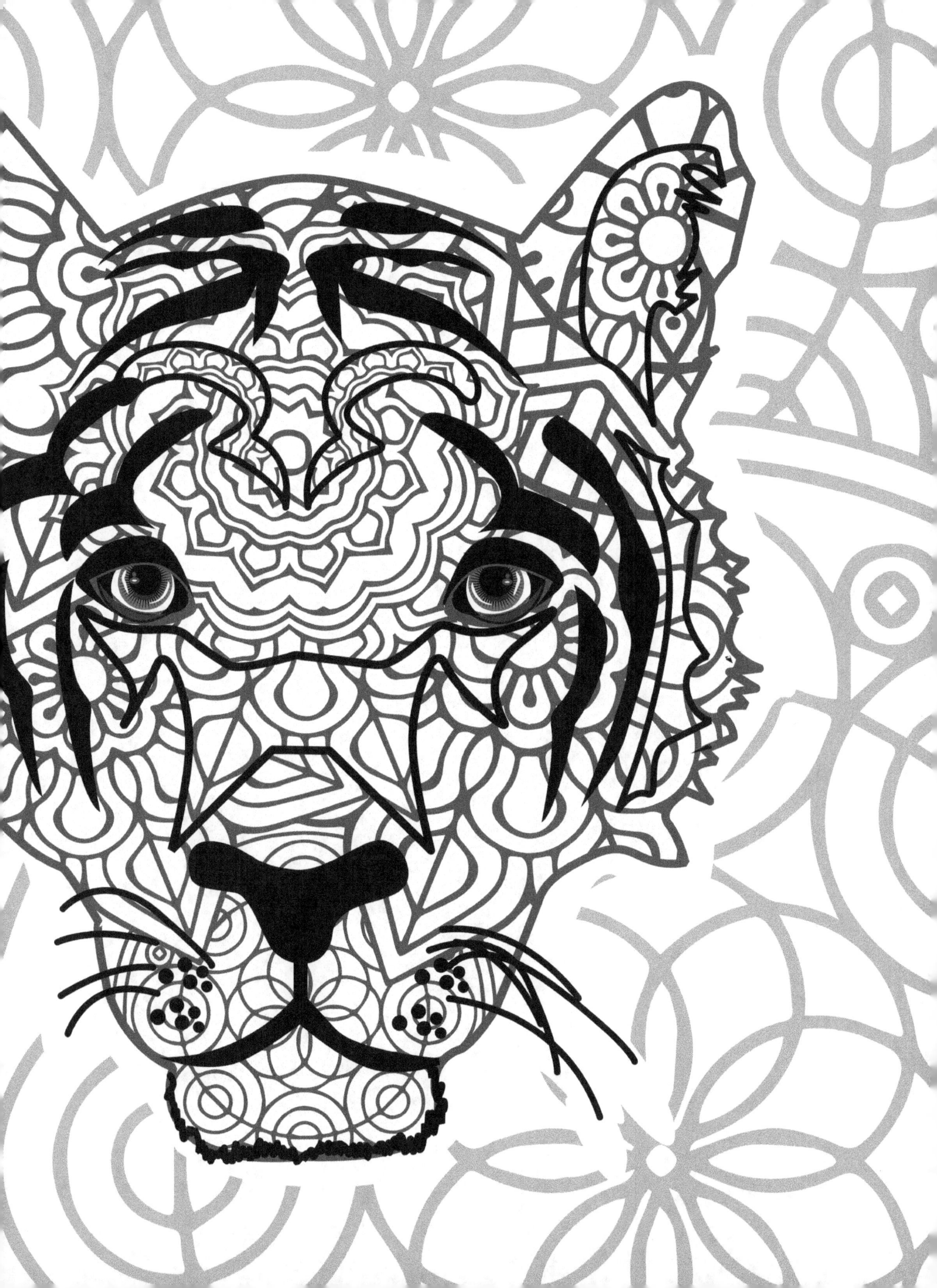

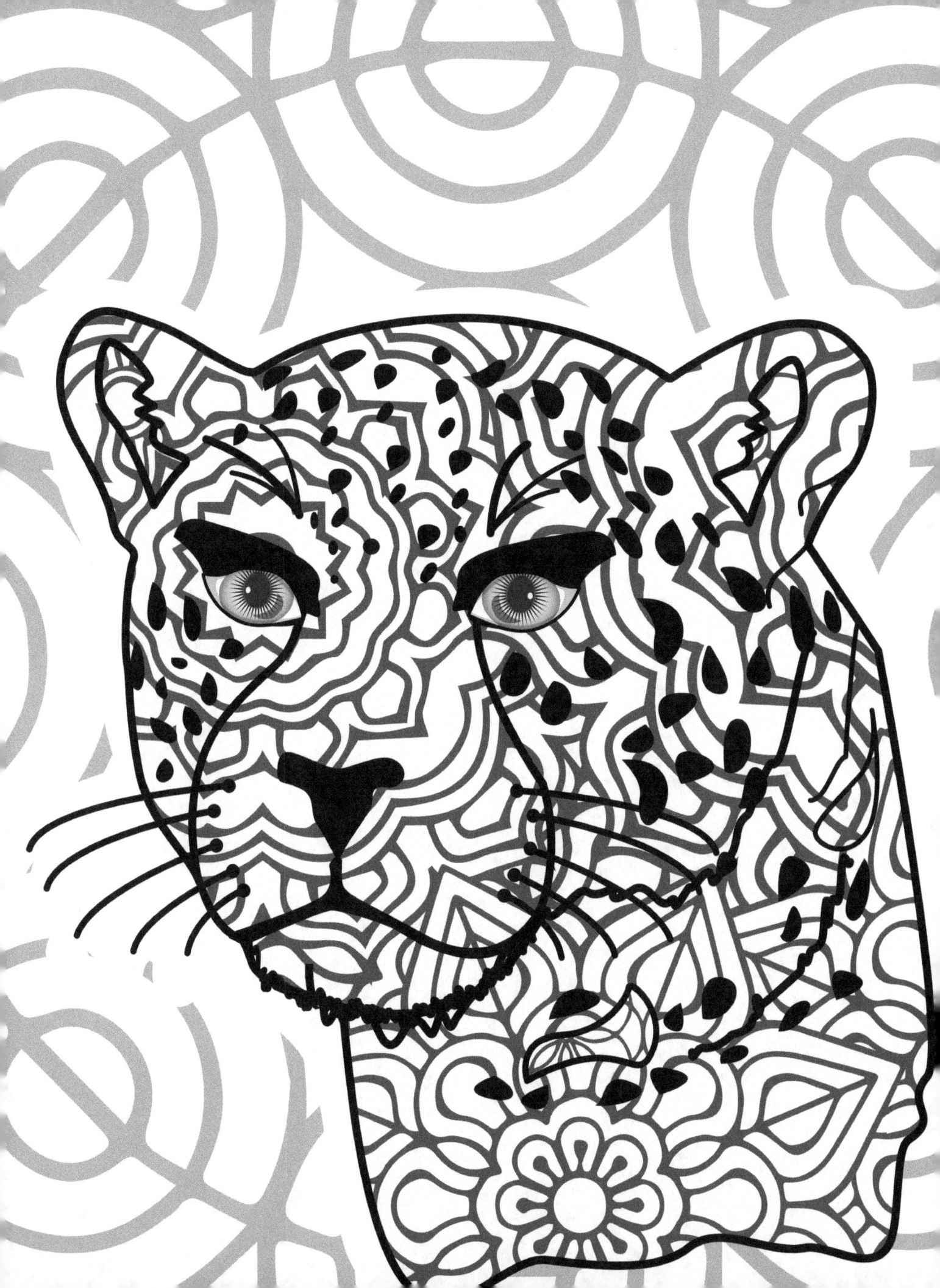

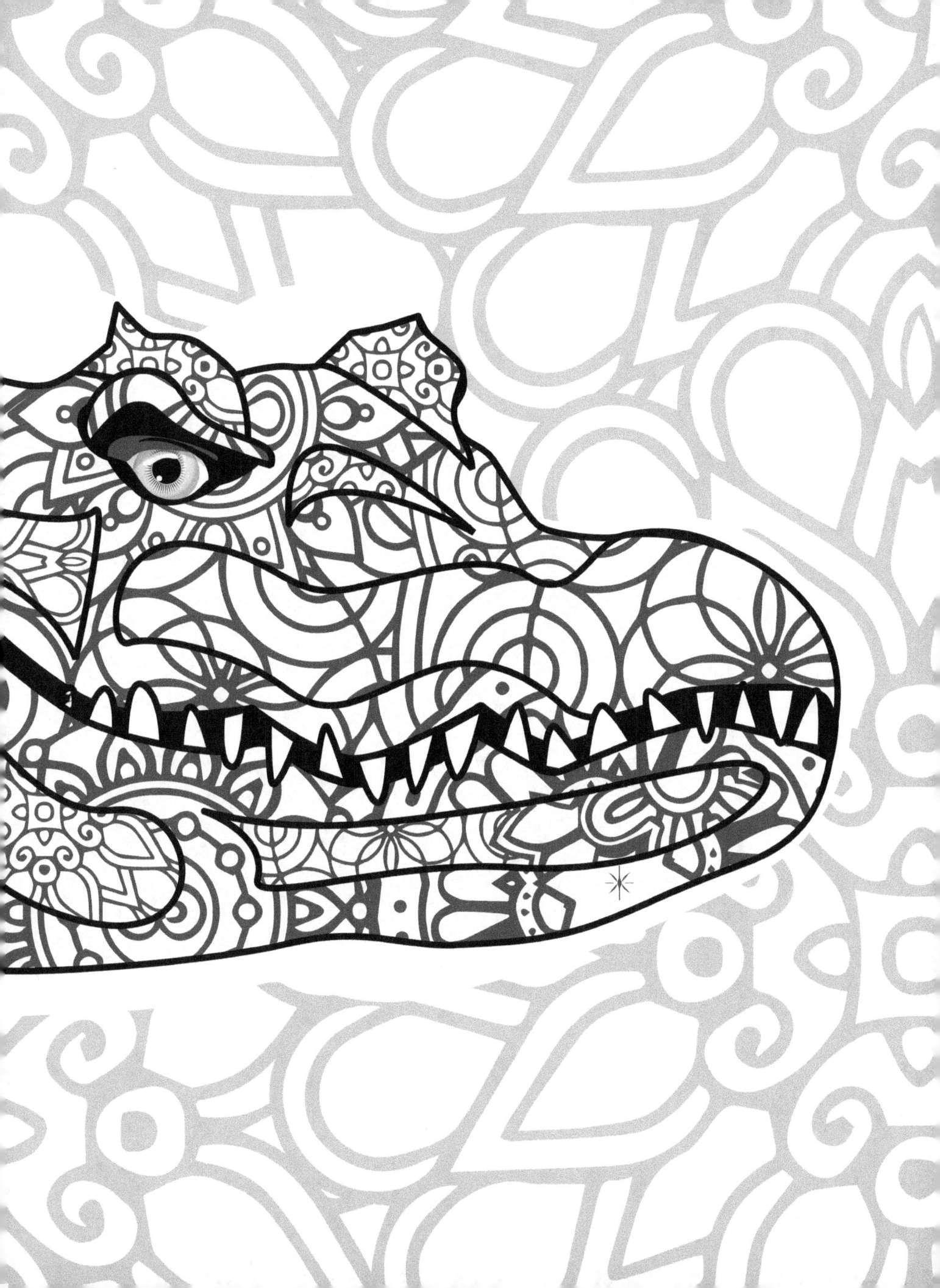

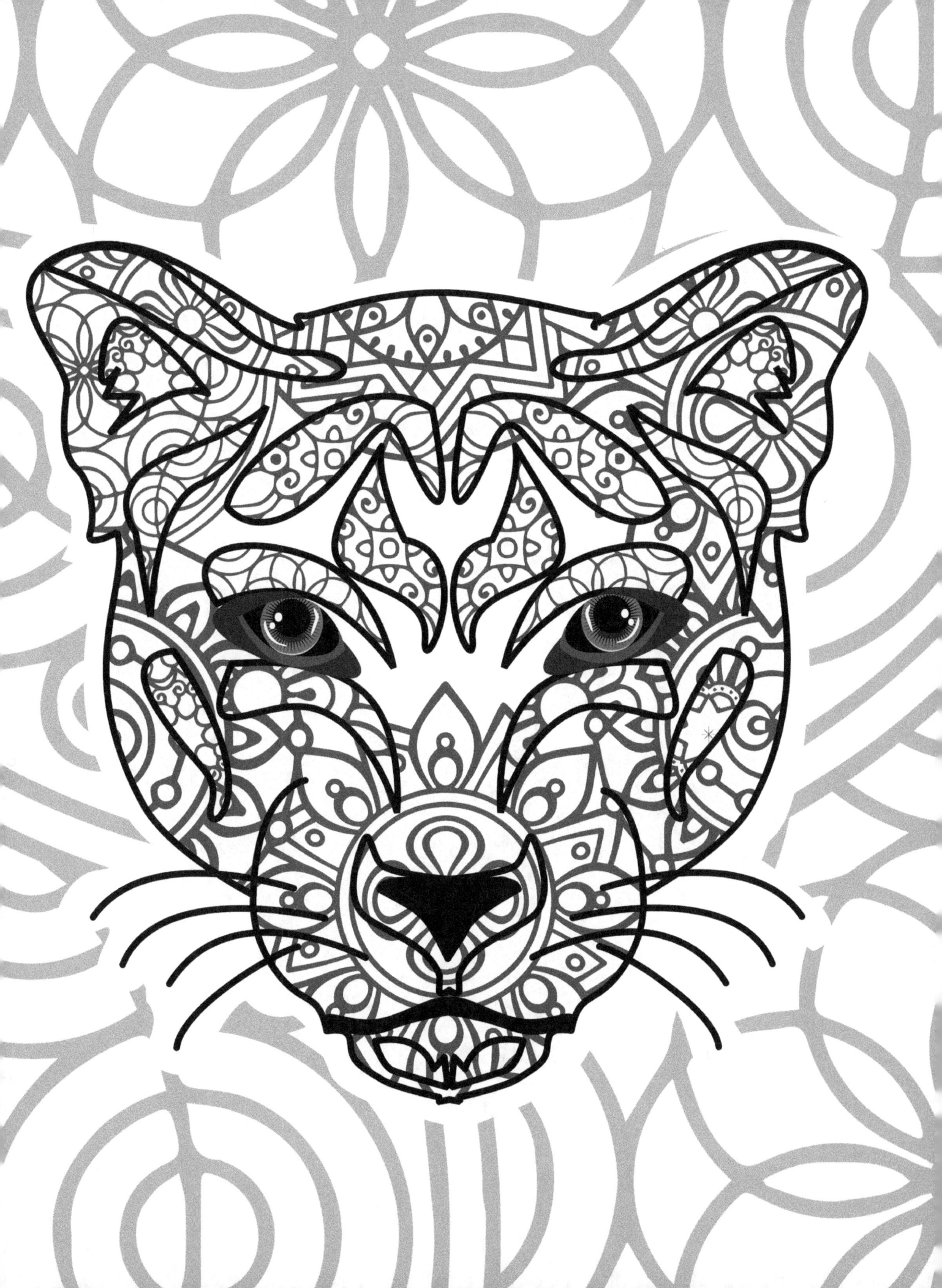

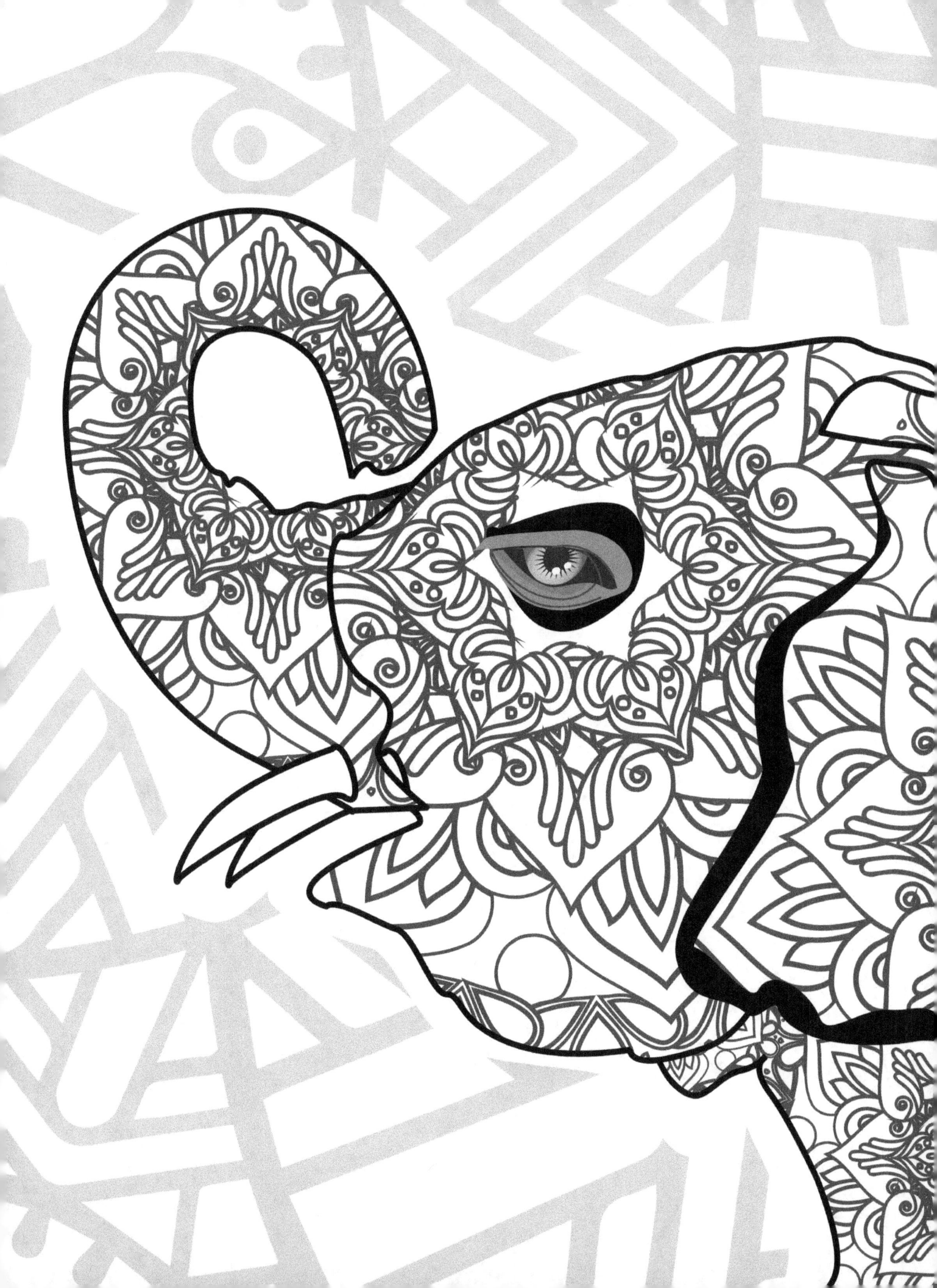

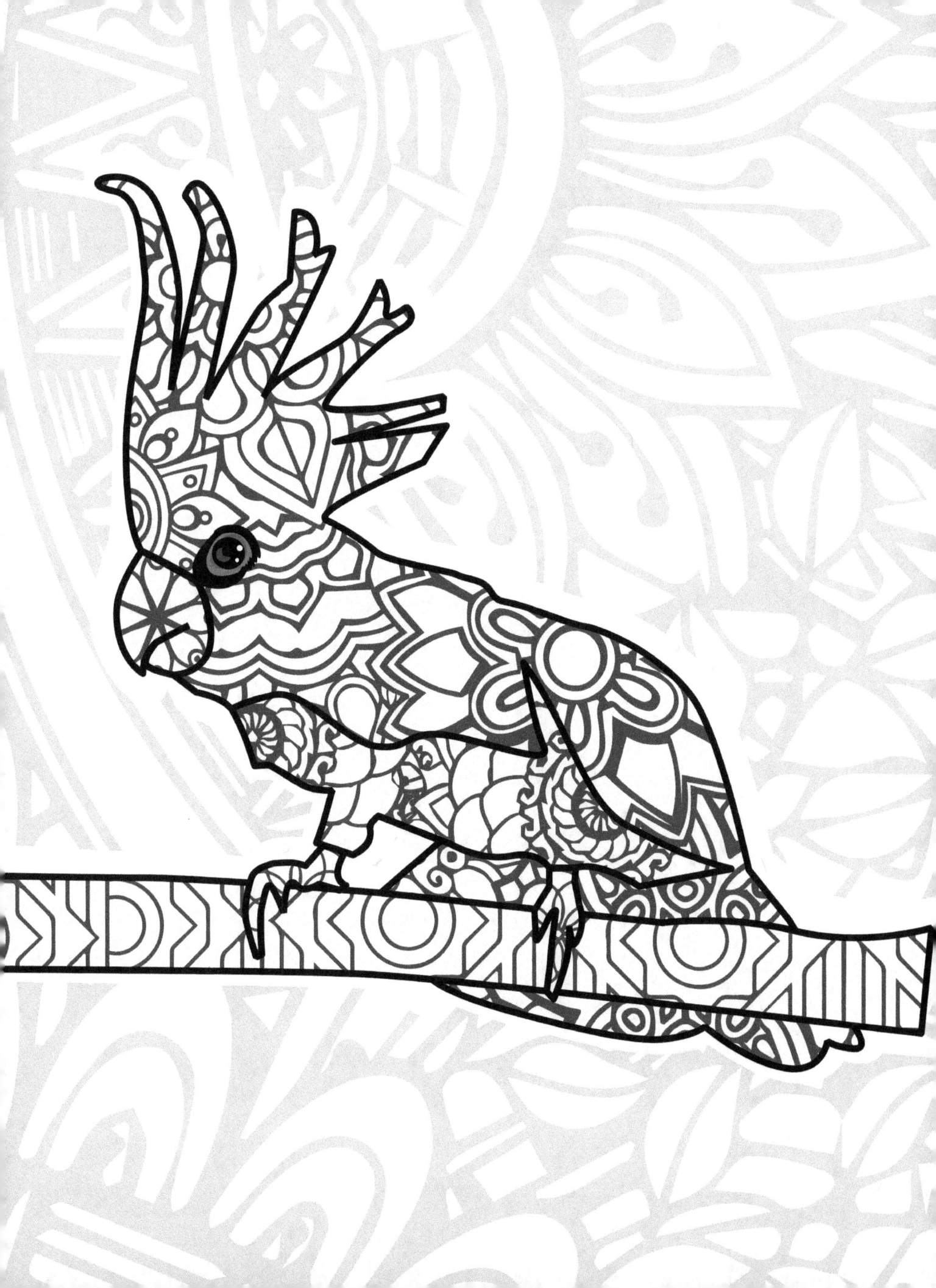

HAKUNA MATATA MADAFAKAS

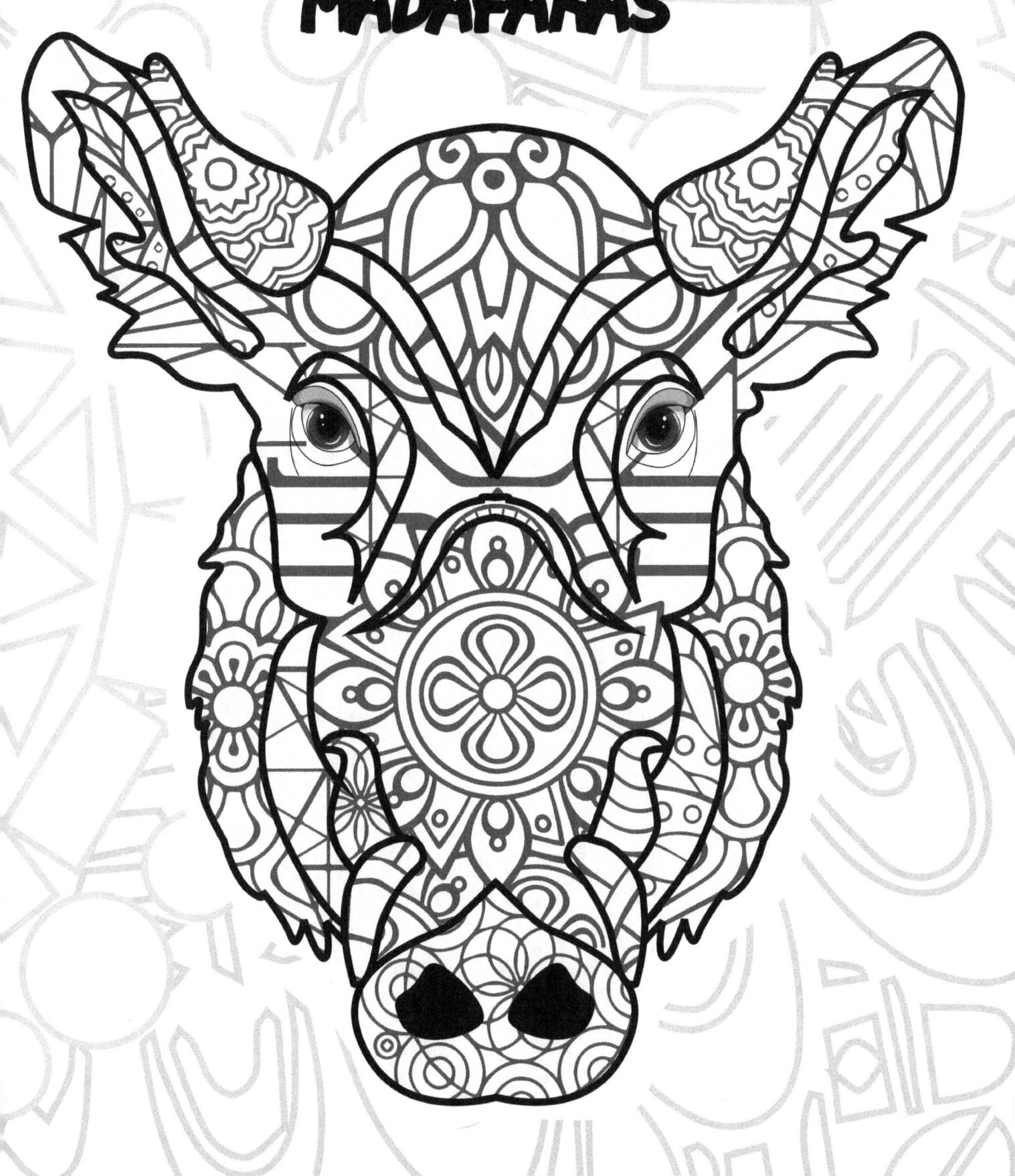

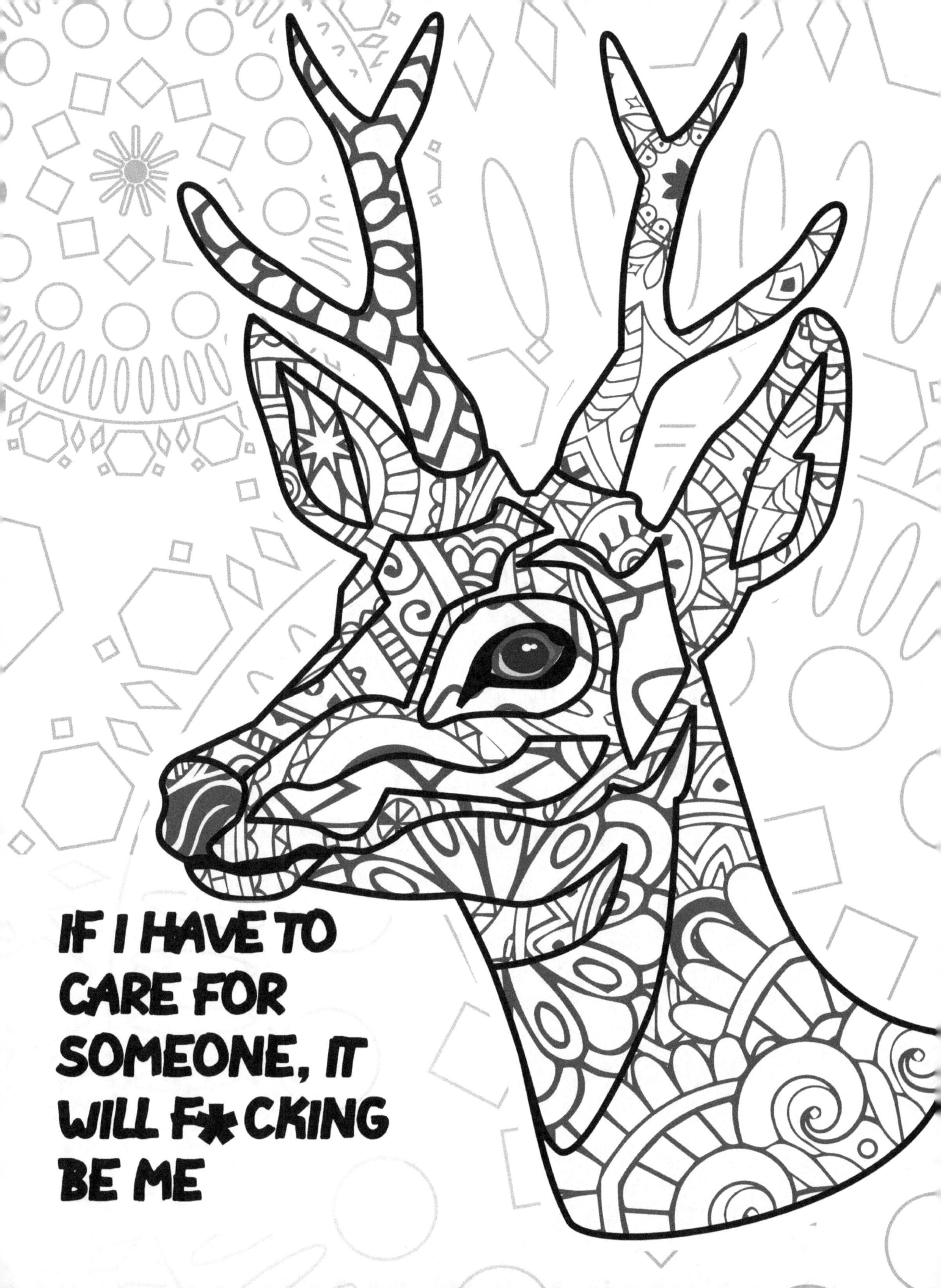

IF I HAVE TO CARE FOR SOMEONE, IT WILL F*CKING BE ME

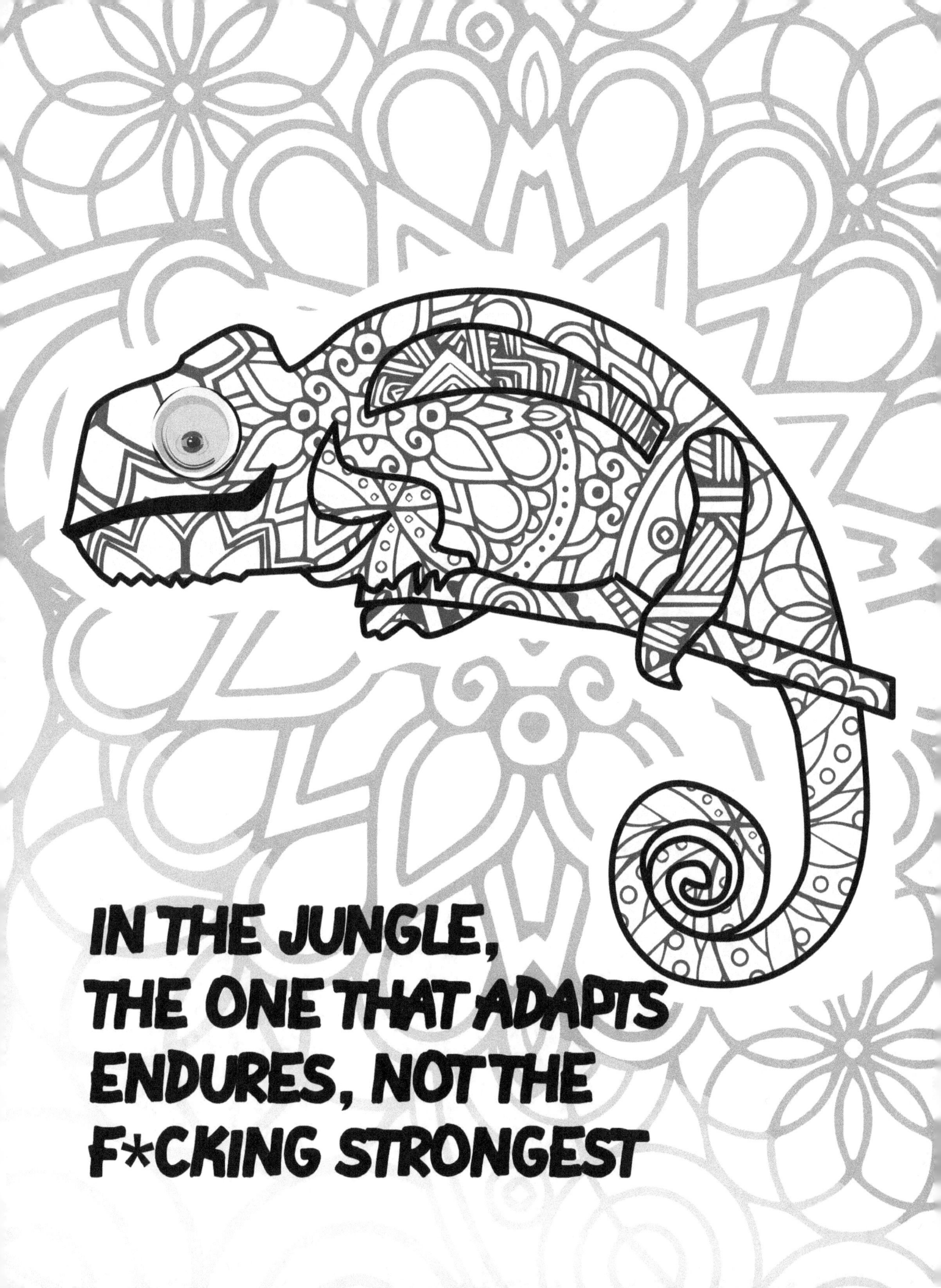

IN THE JUNGLE,
THE ONE THAT ADAPTS
ENDURES, NOT THE
F*CKING STRONGEST

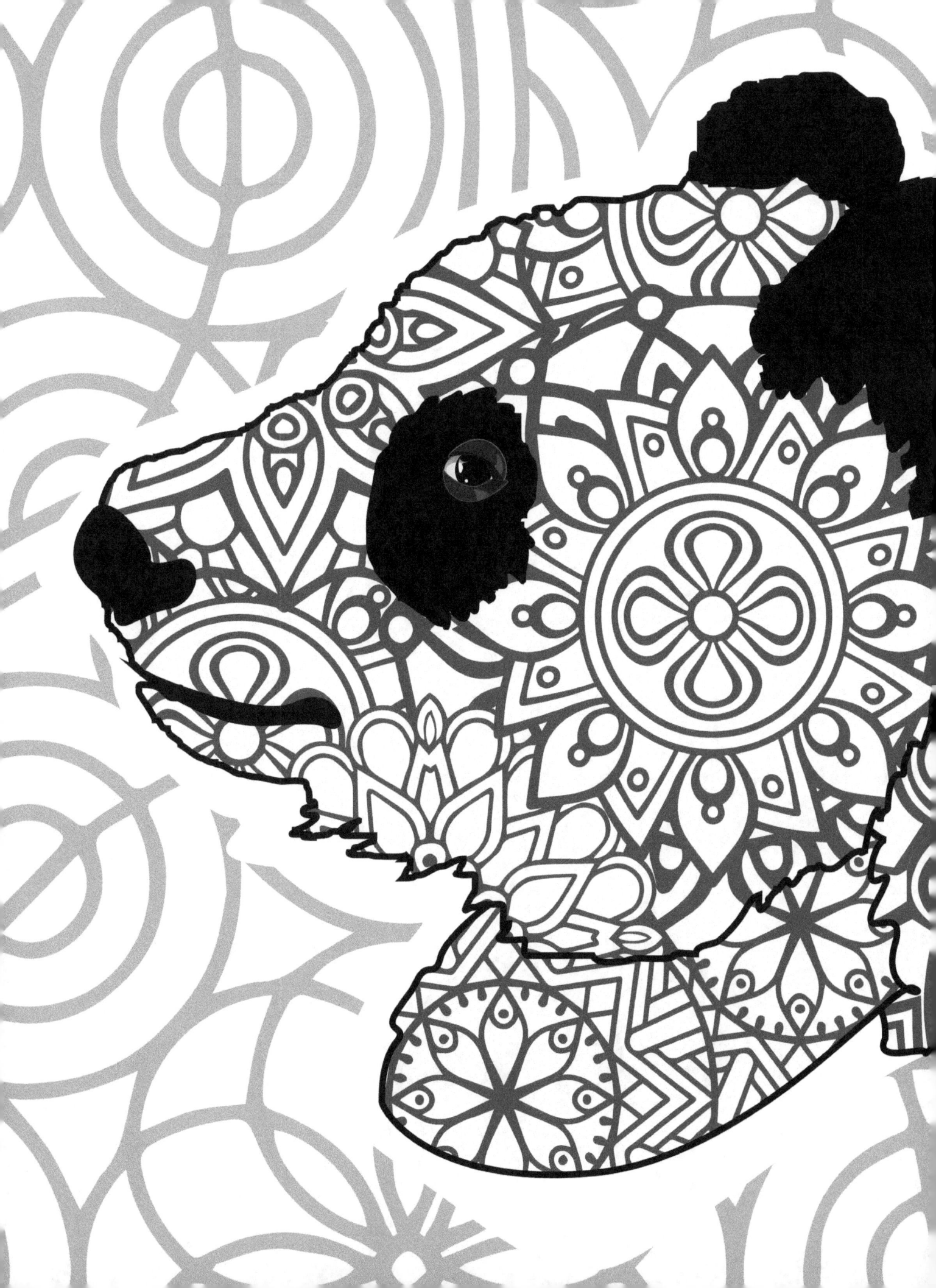

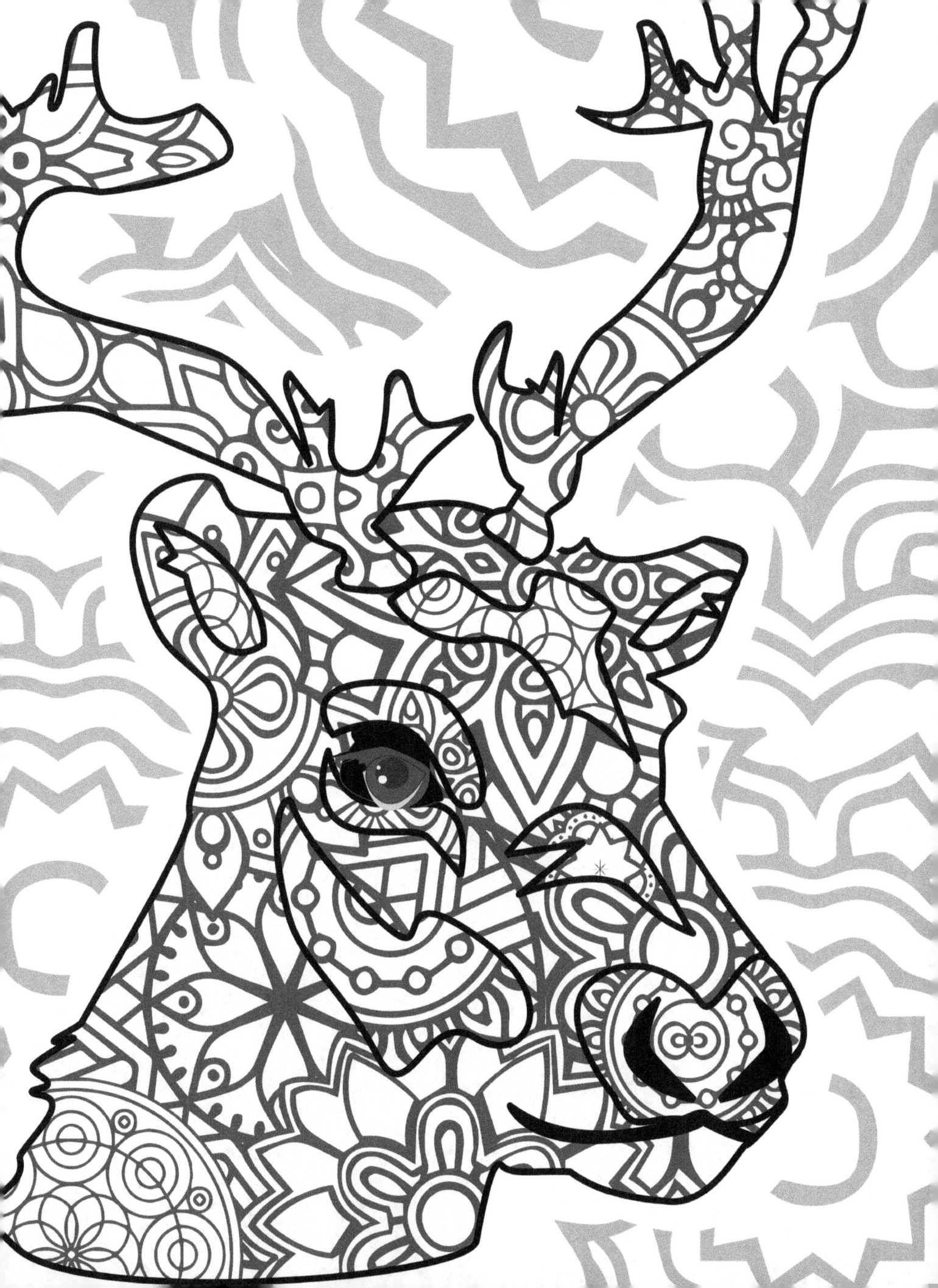

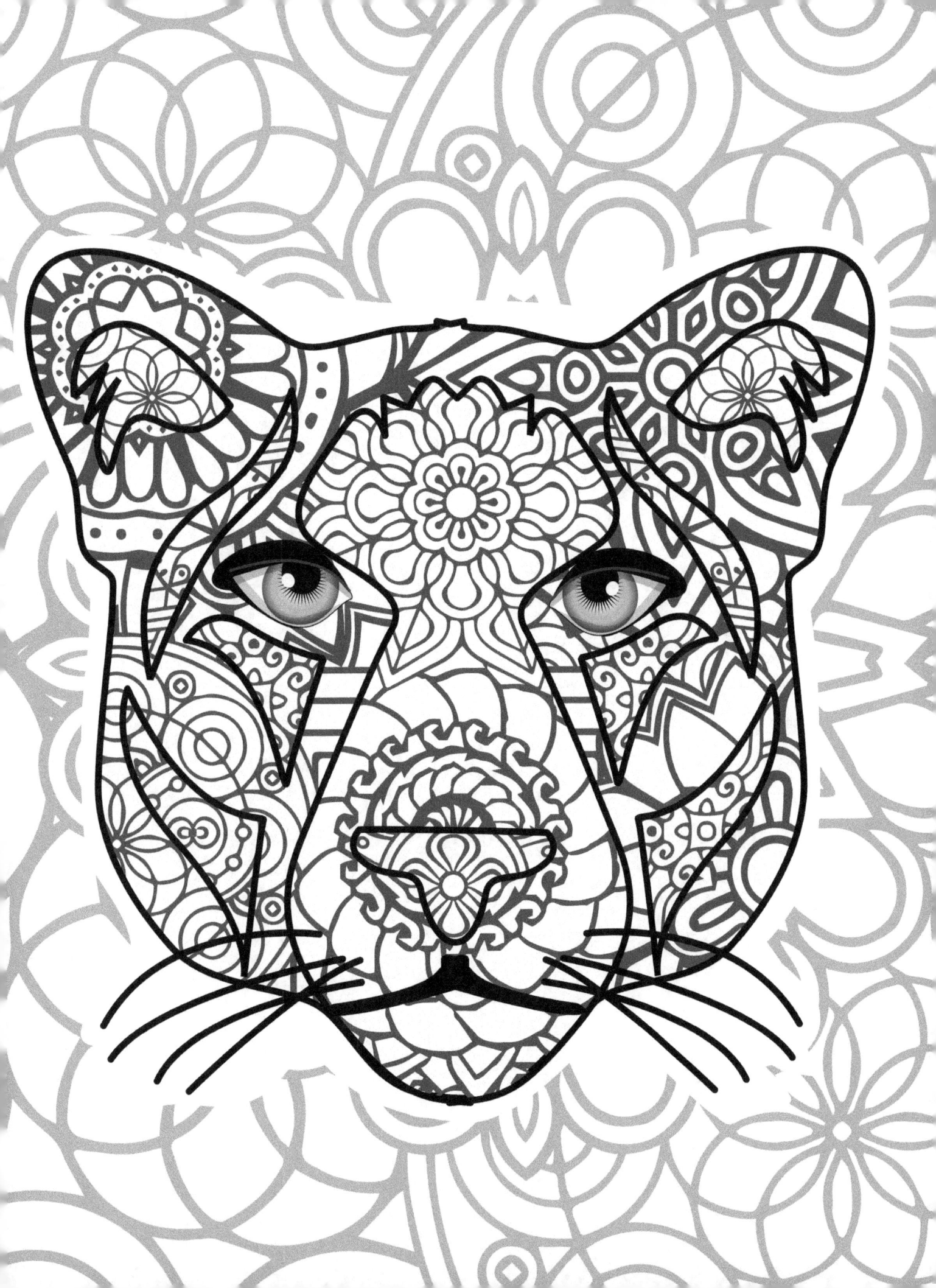

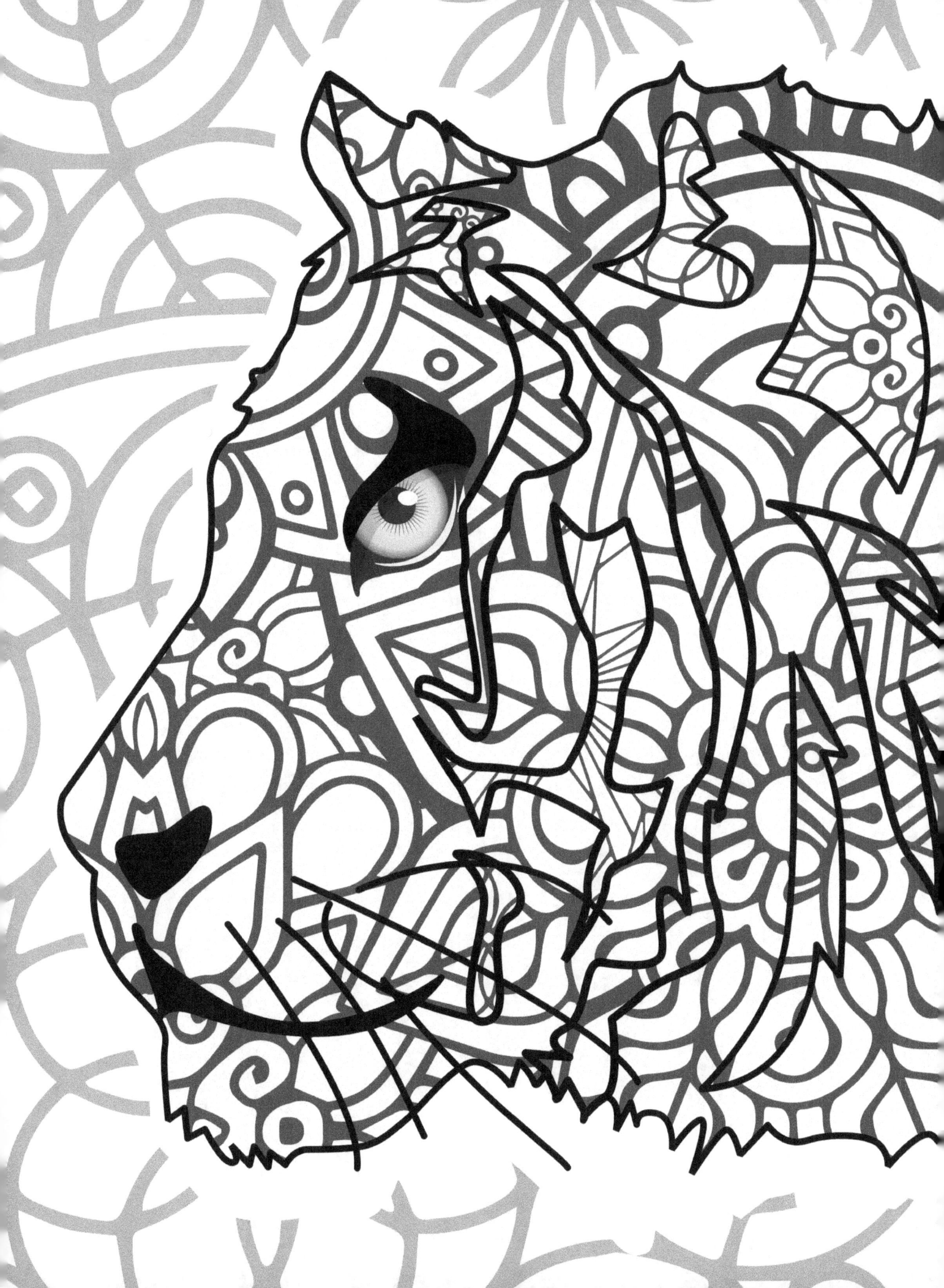

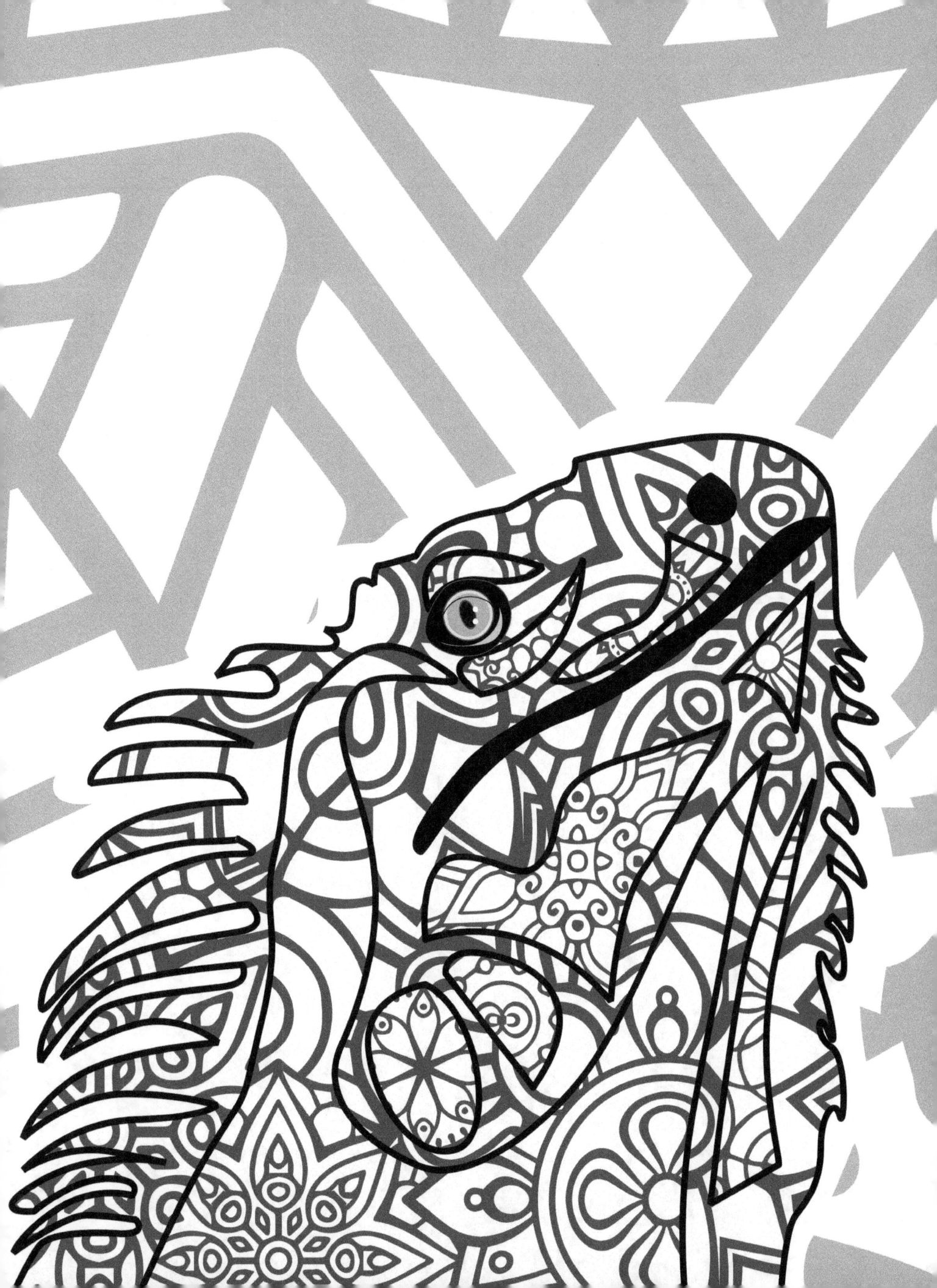

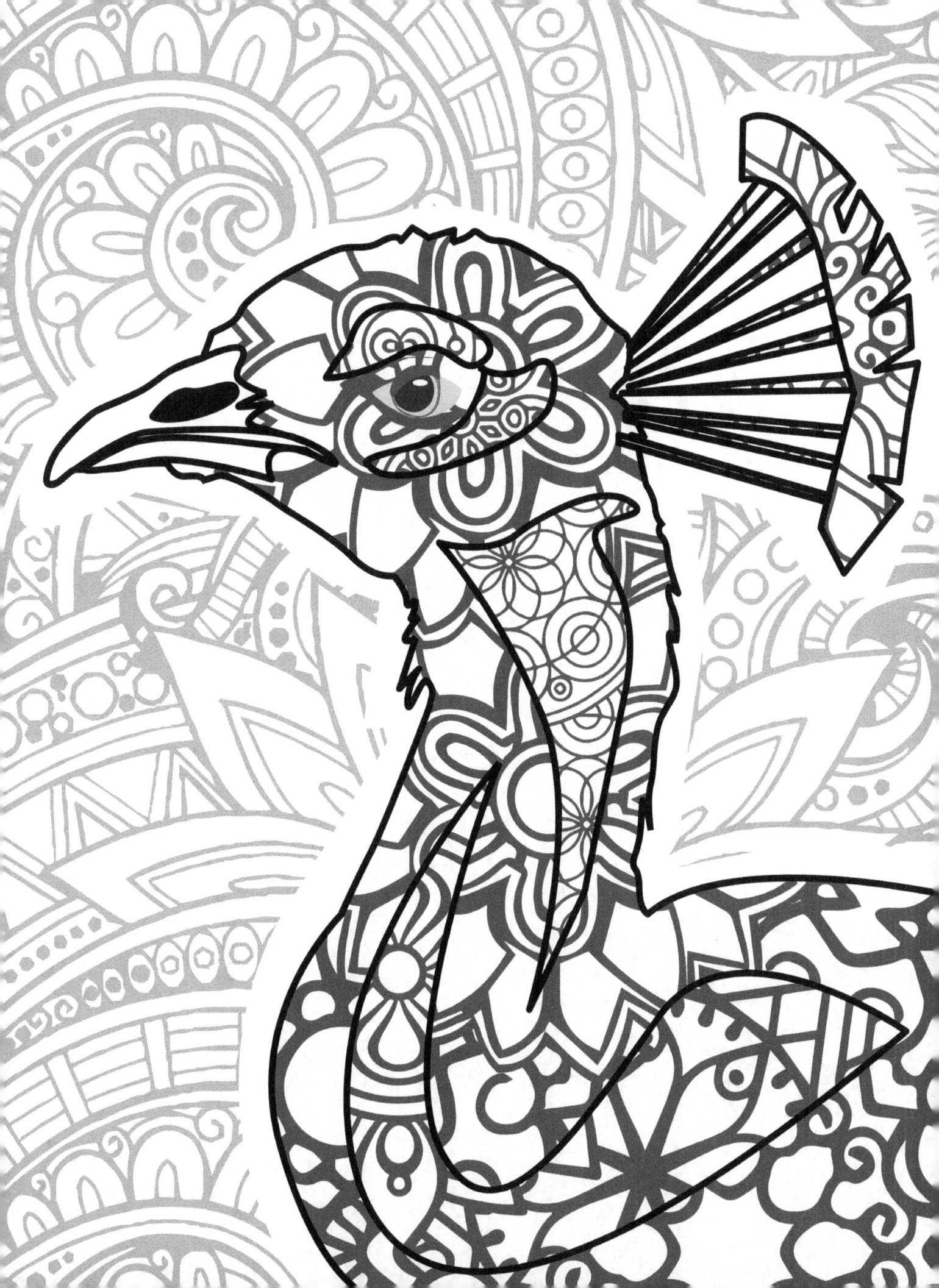

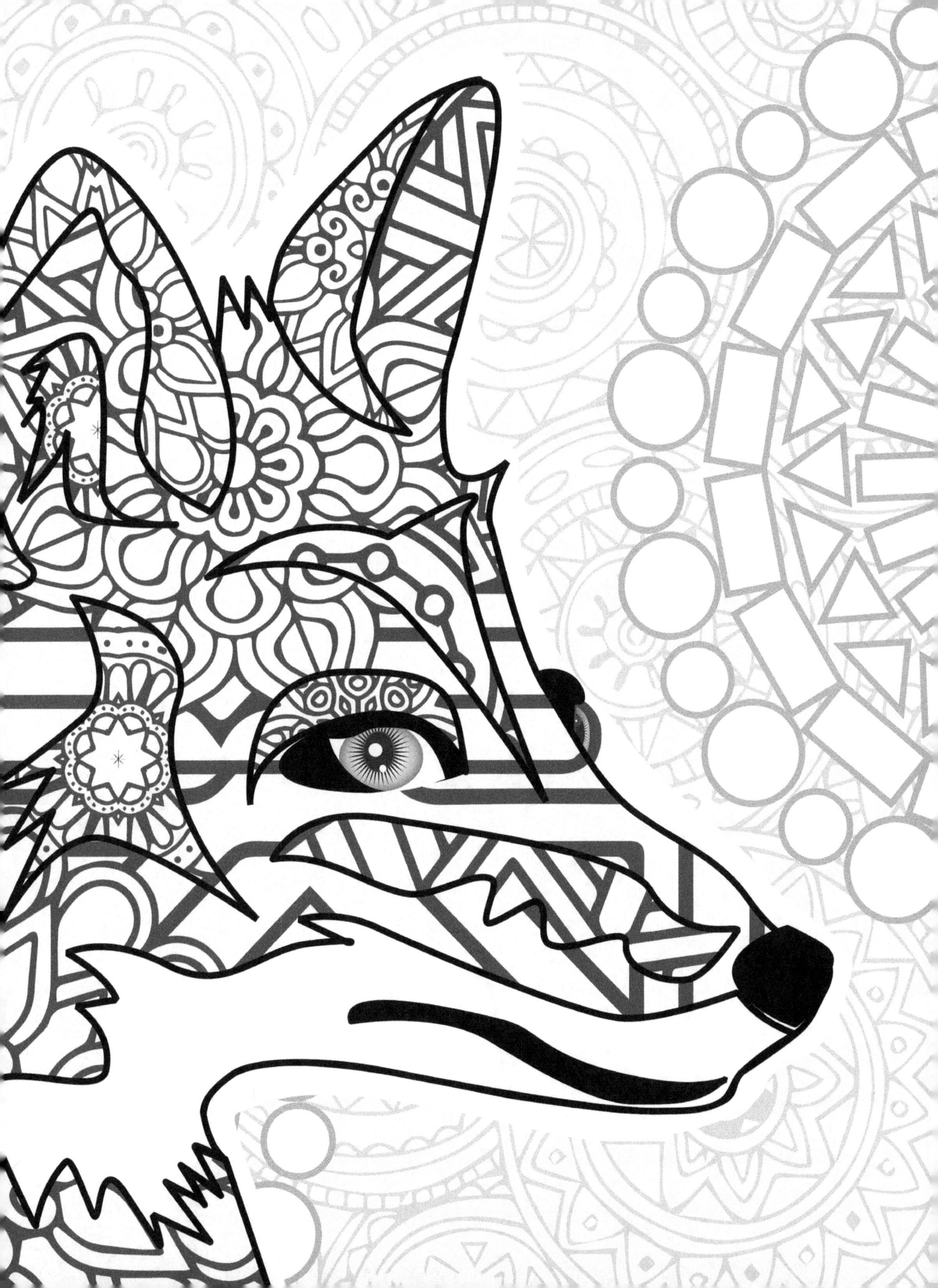

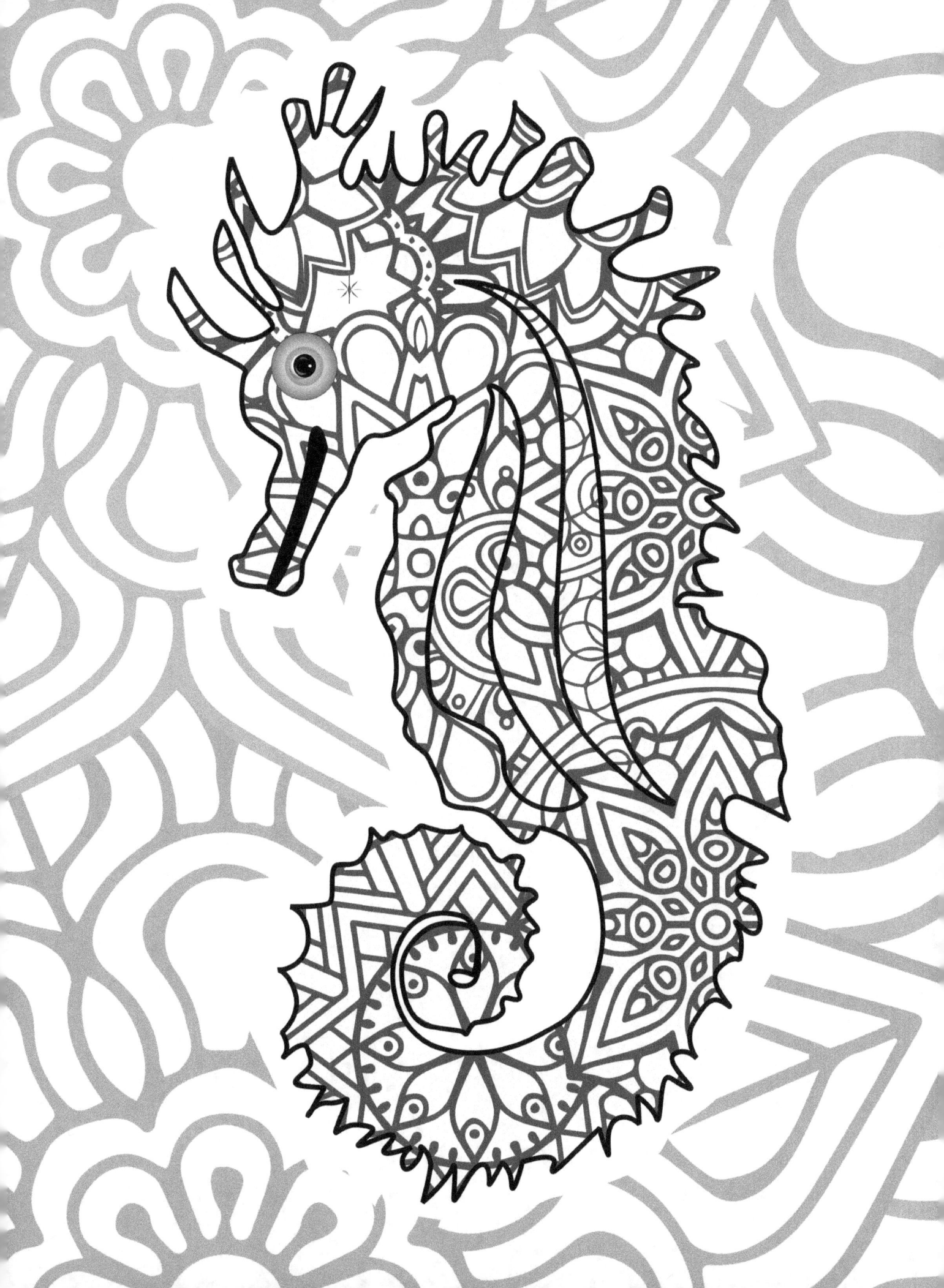

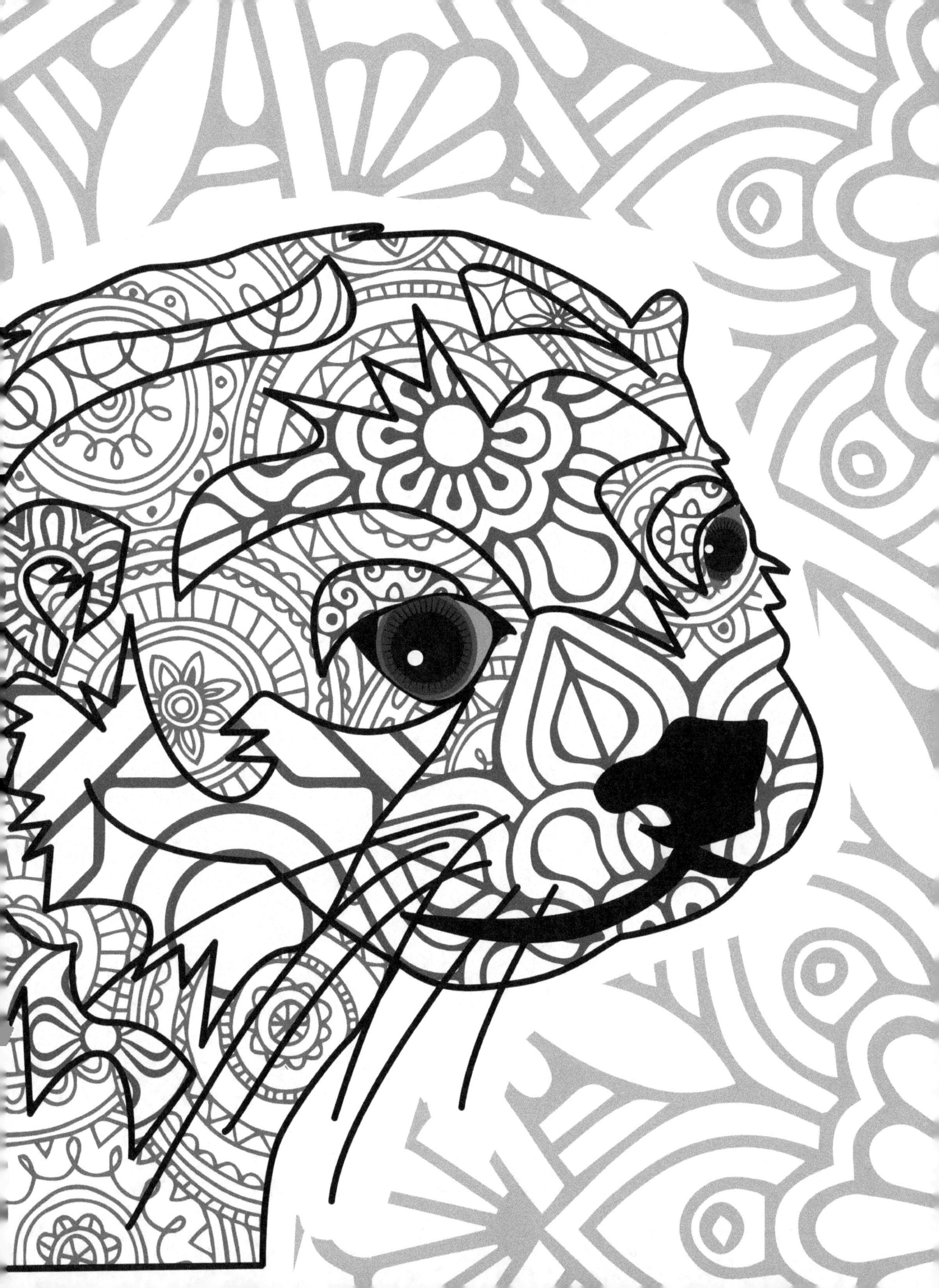

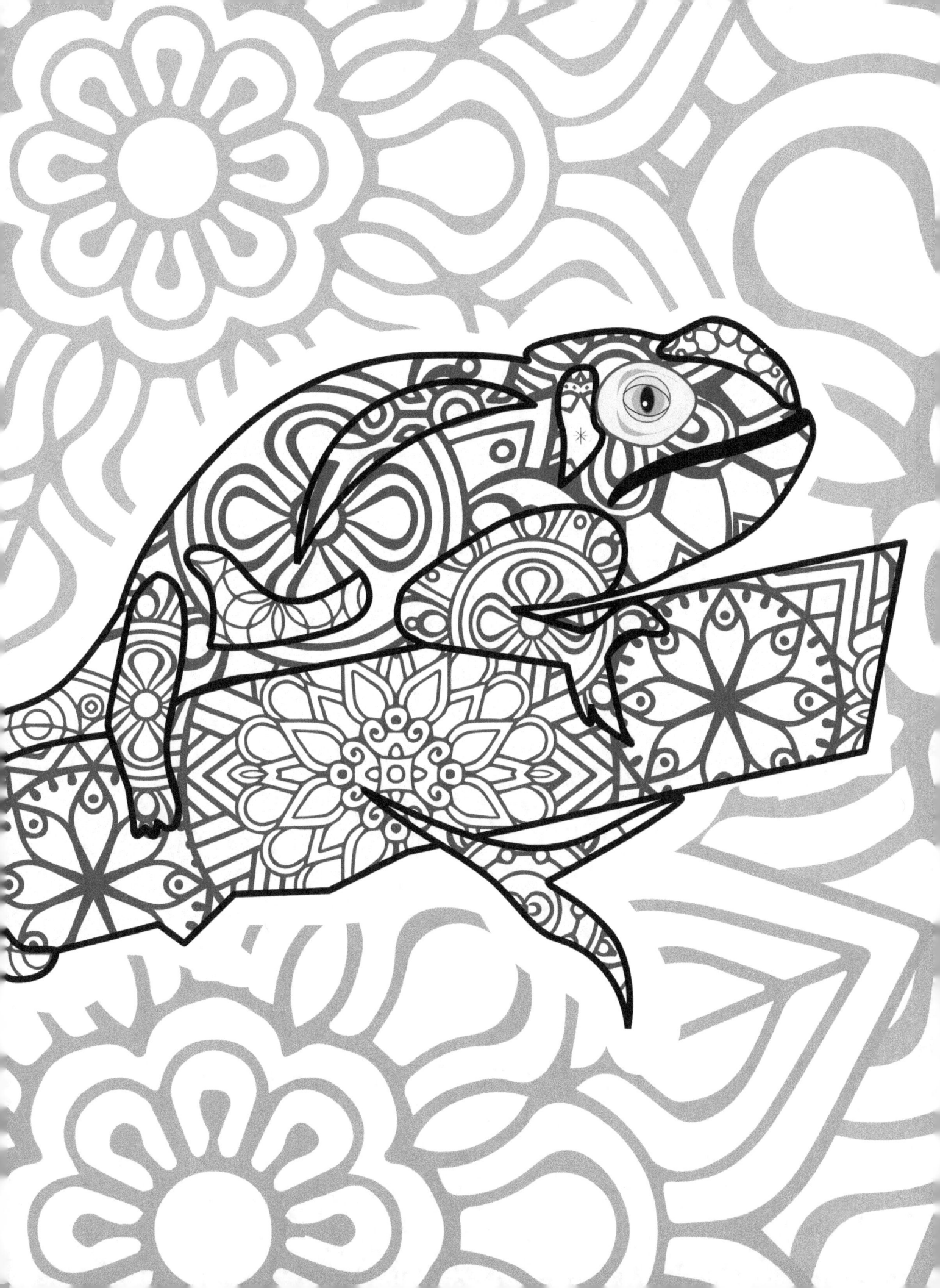

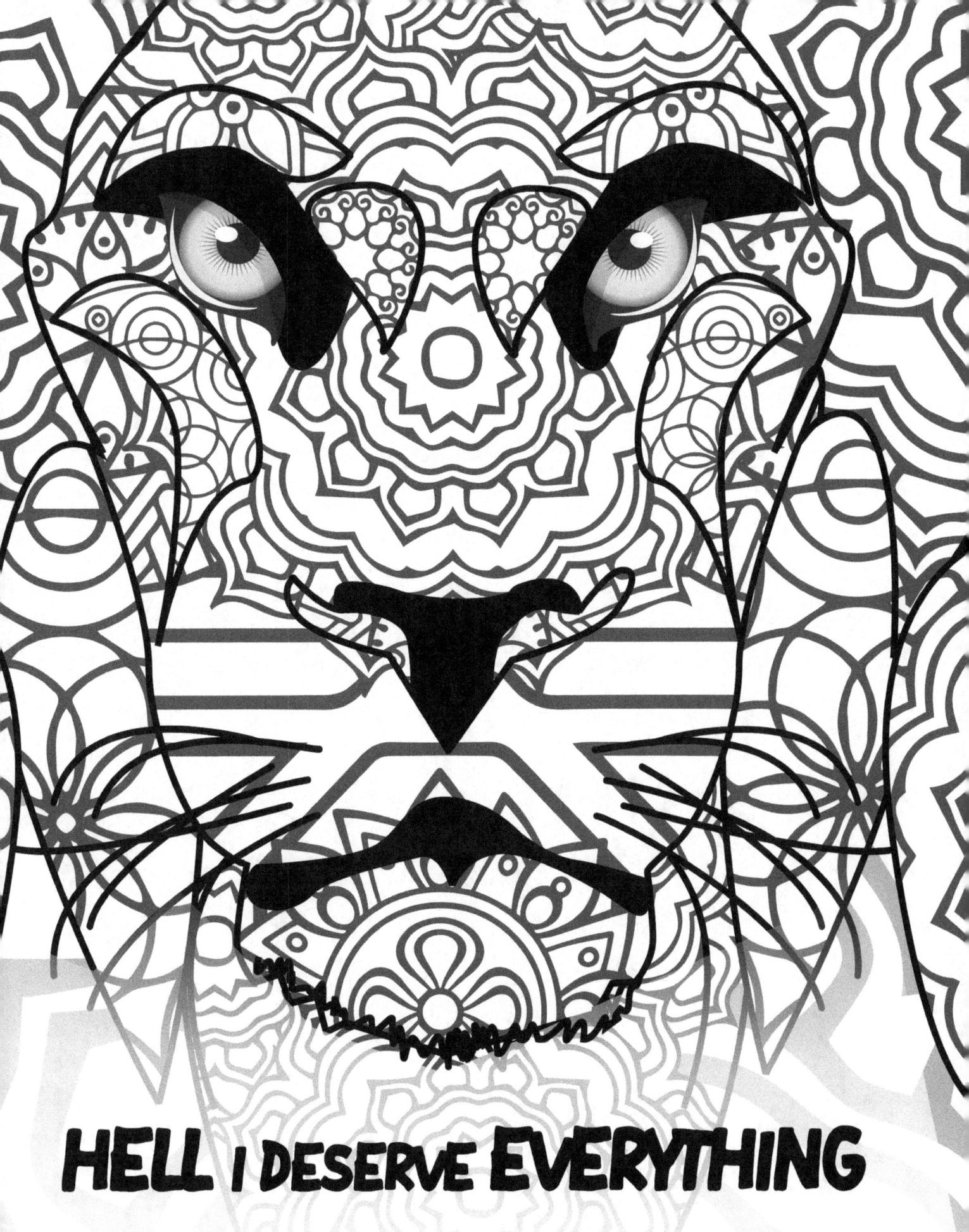

HELL I DESERVE EVERYTHING

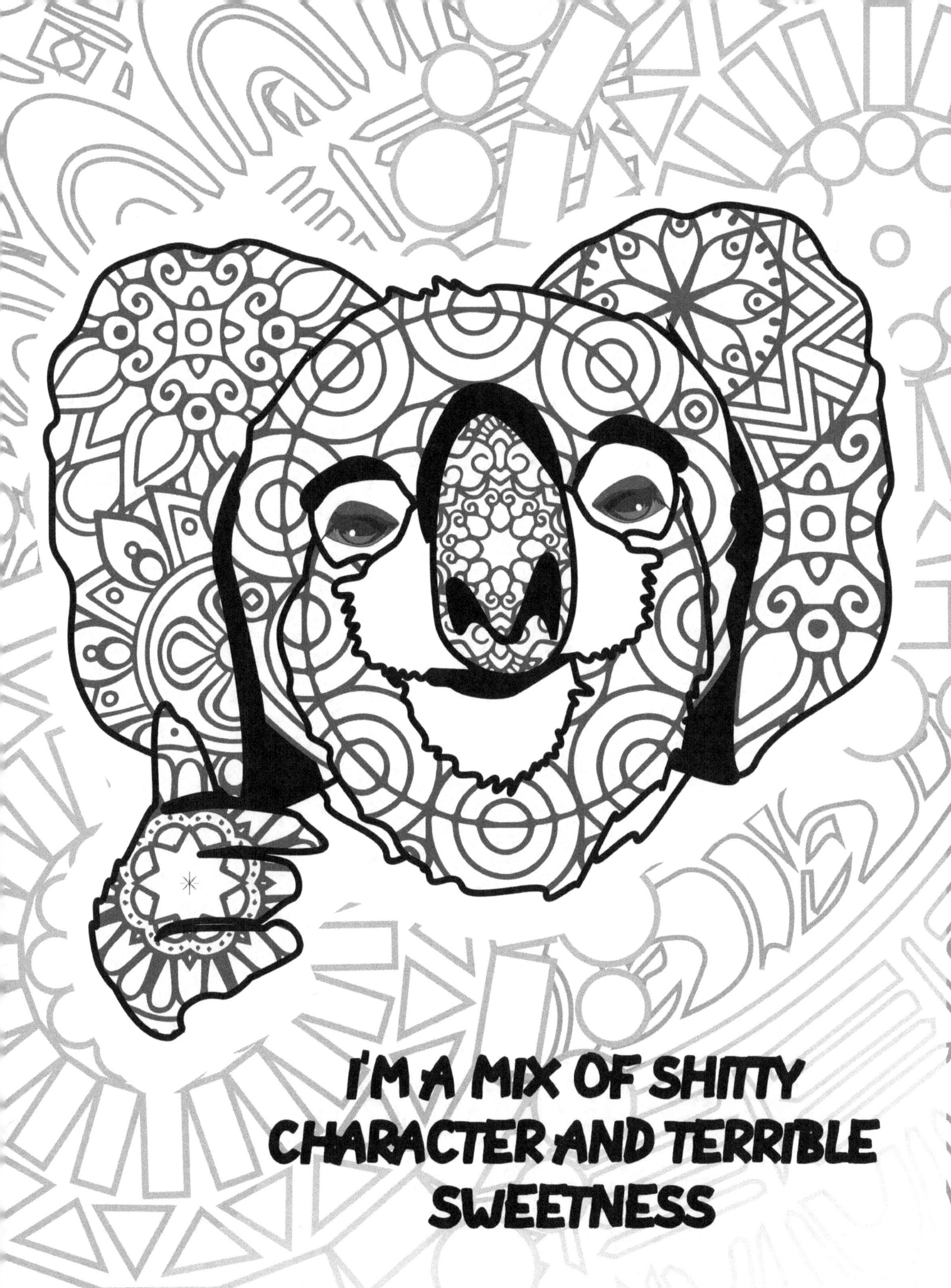

I'M A MIX OF SHITTY CHARACTER AND TERRIBLE SWEETNESS

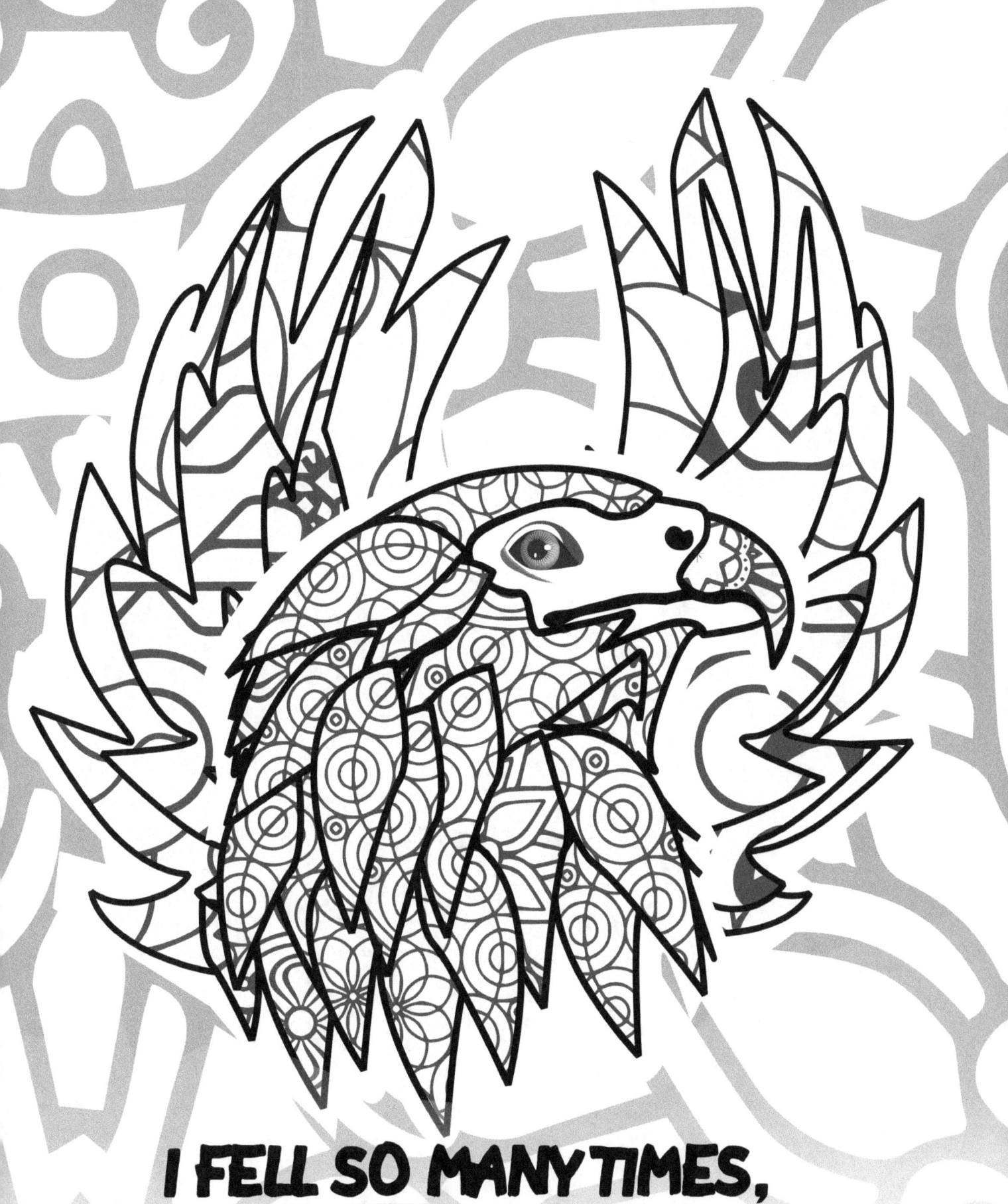

I FELL SO MANY TIMES,
HELL I LEARNED HOW TO FLY

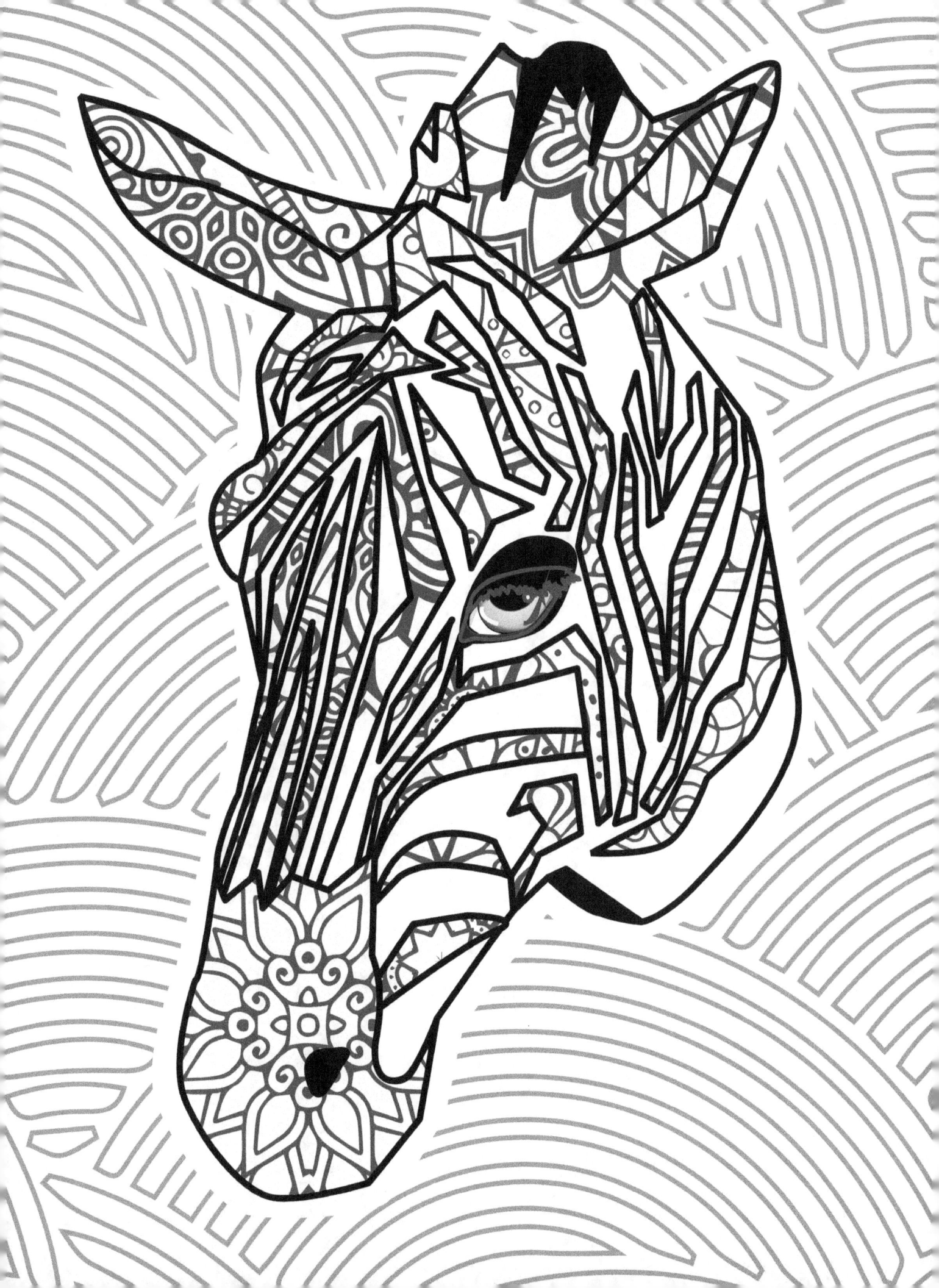

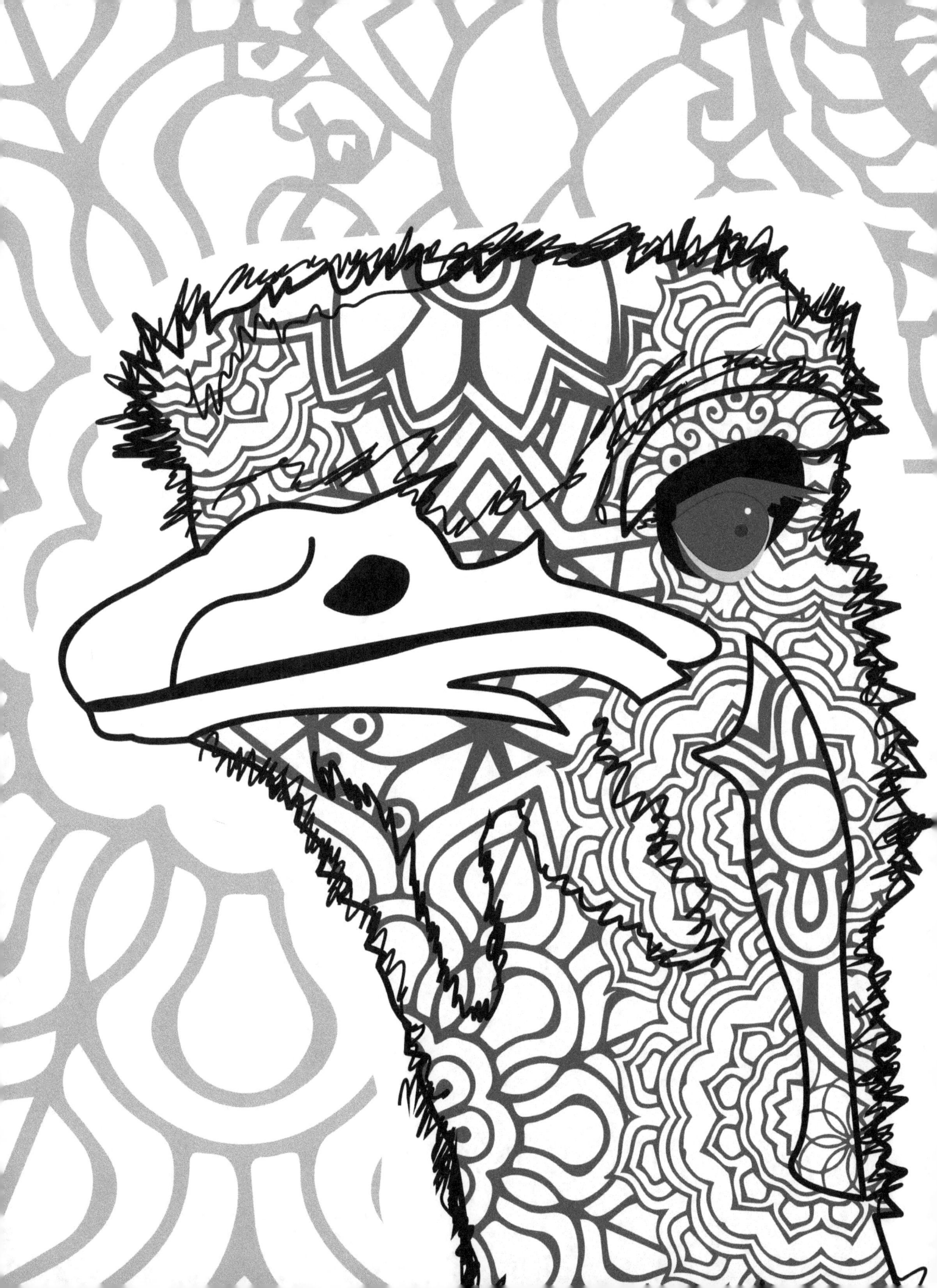

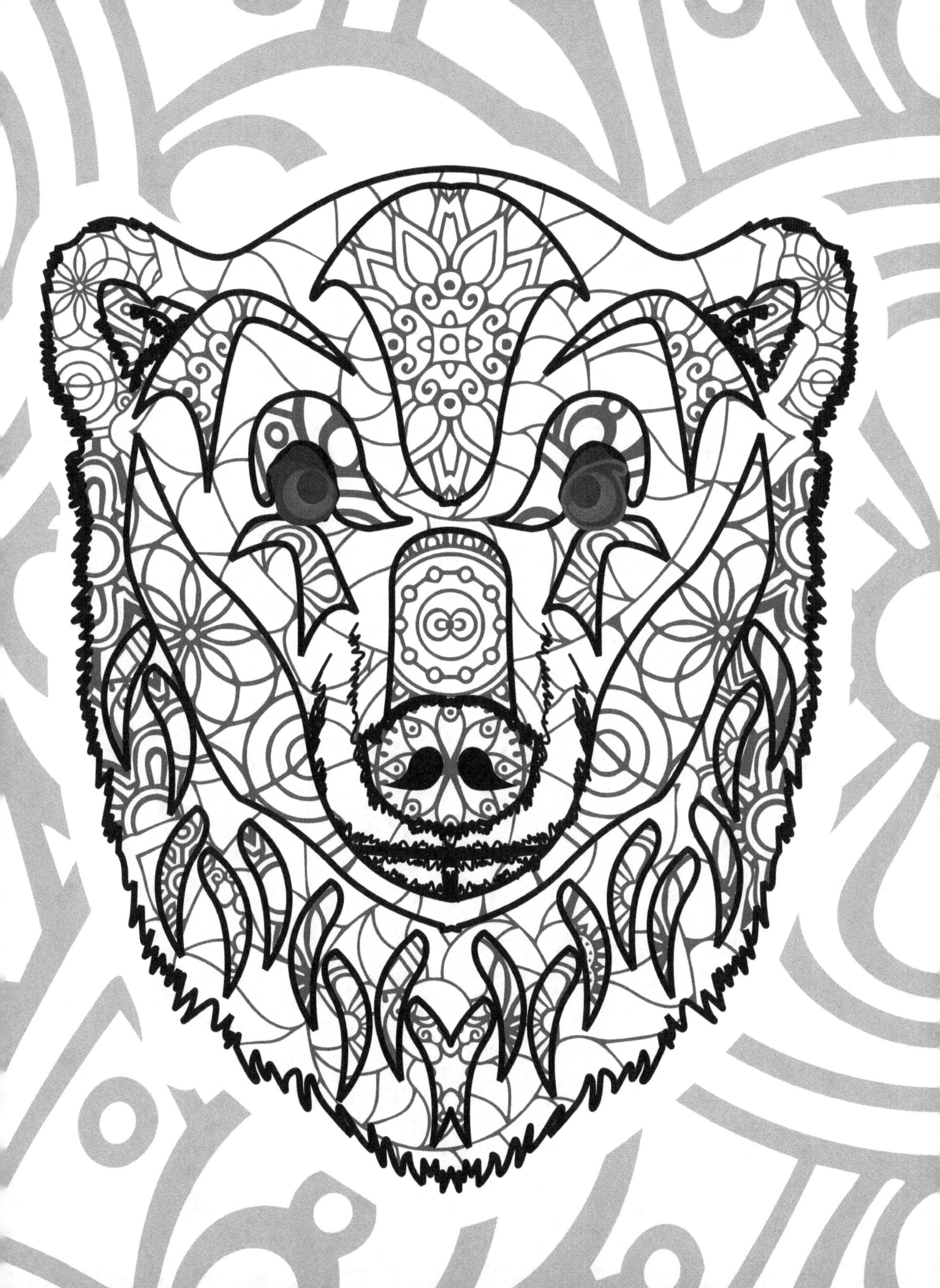

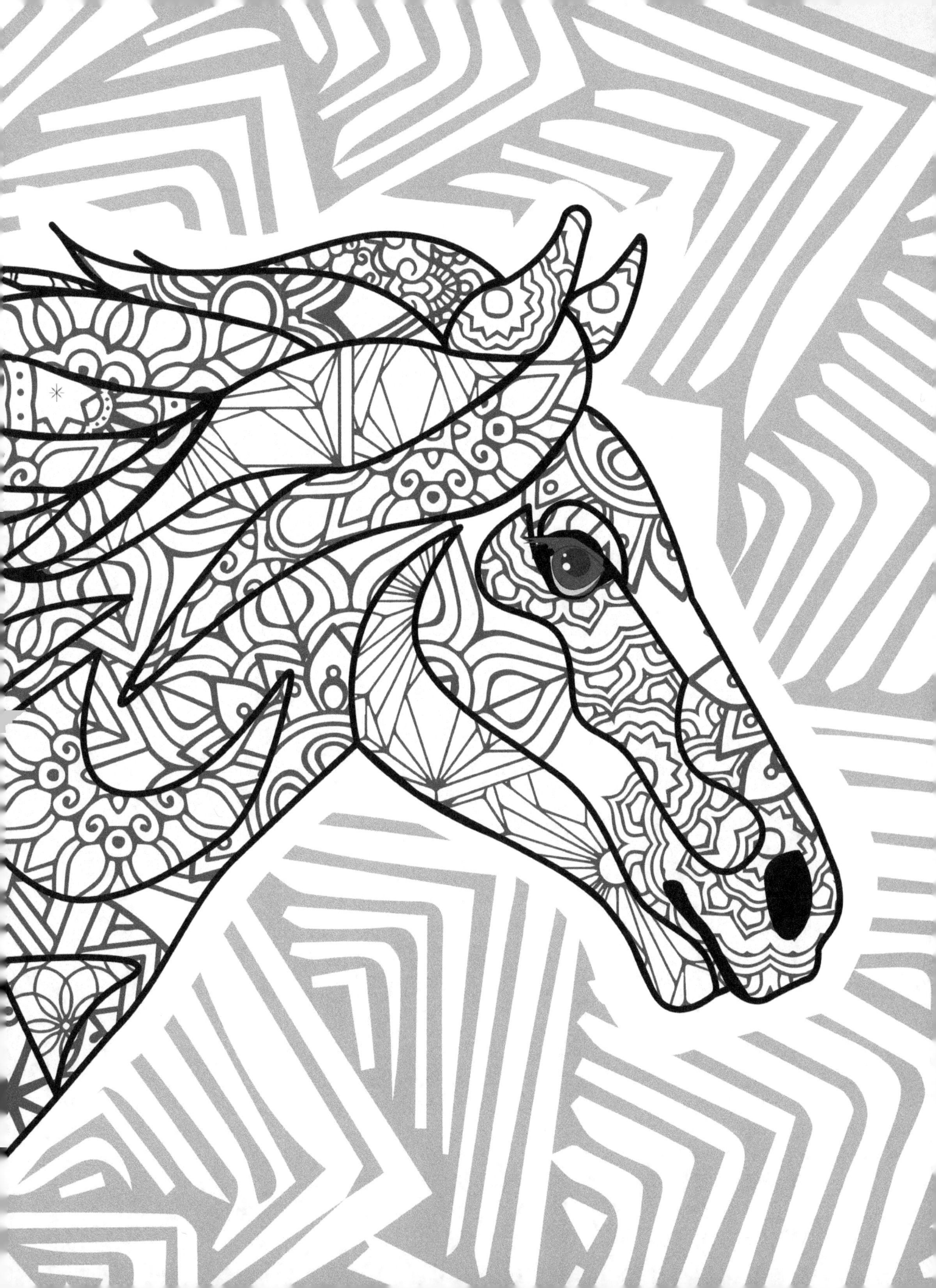

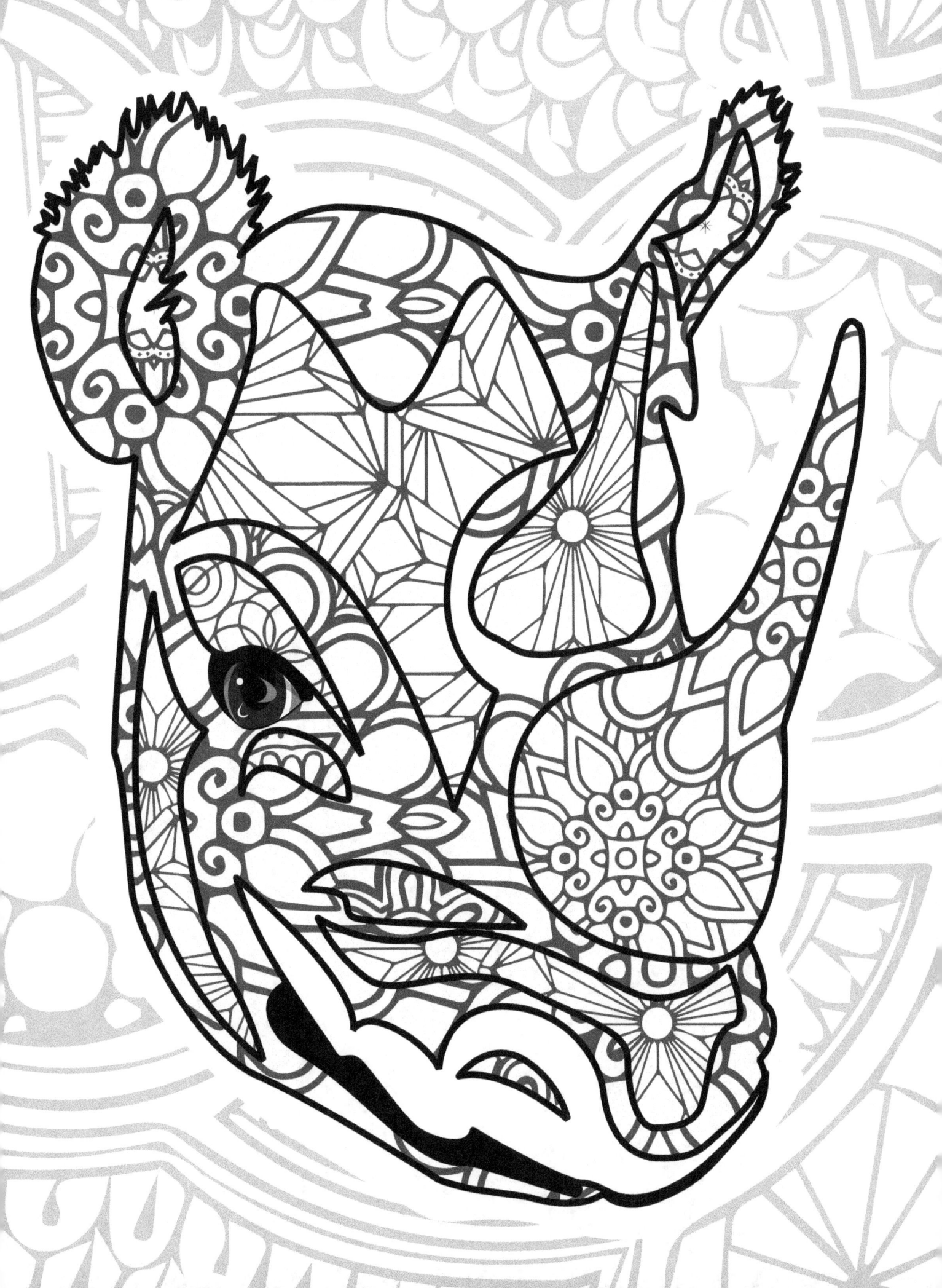

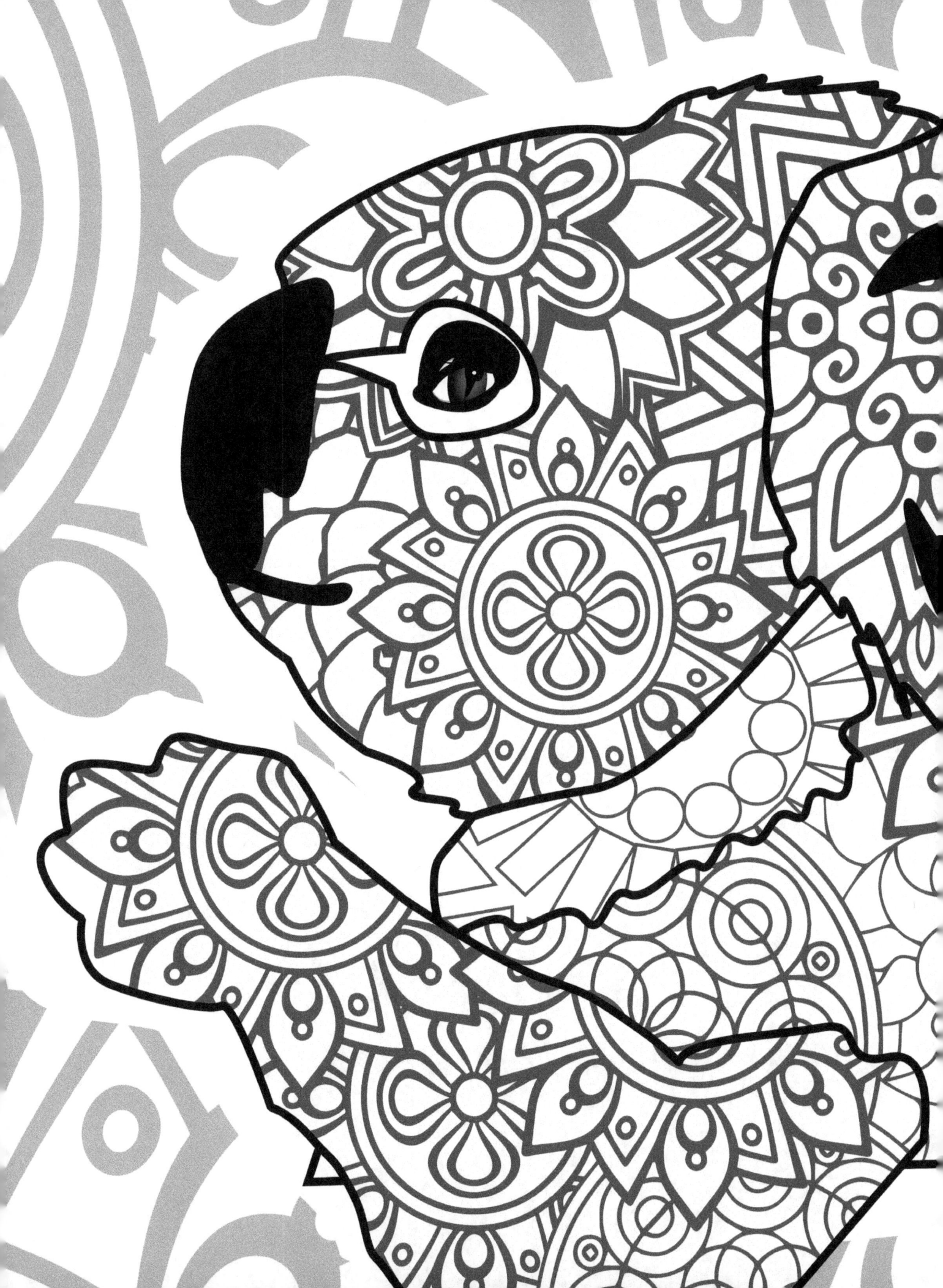

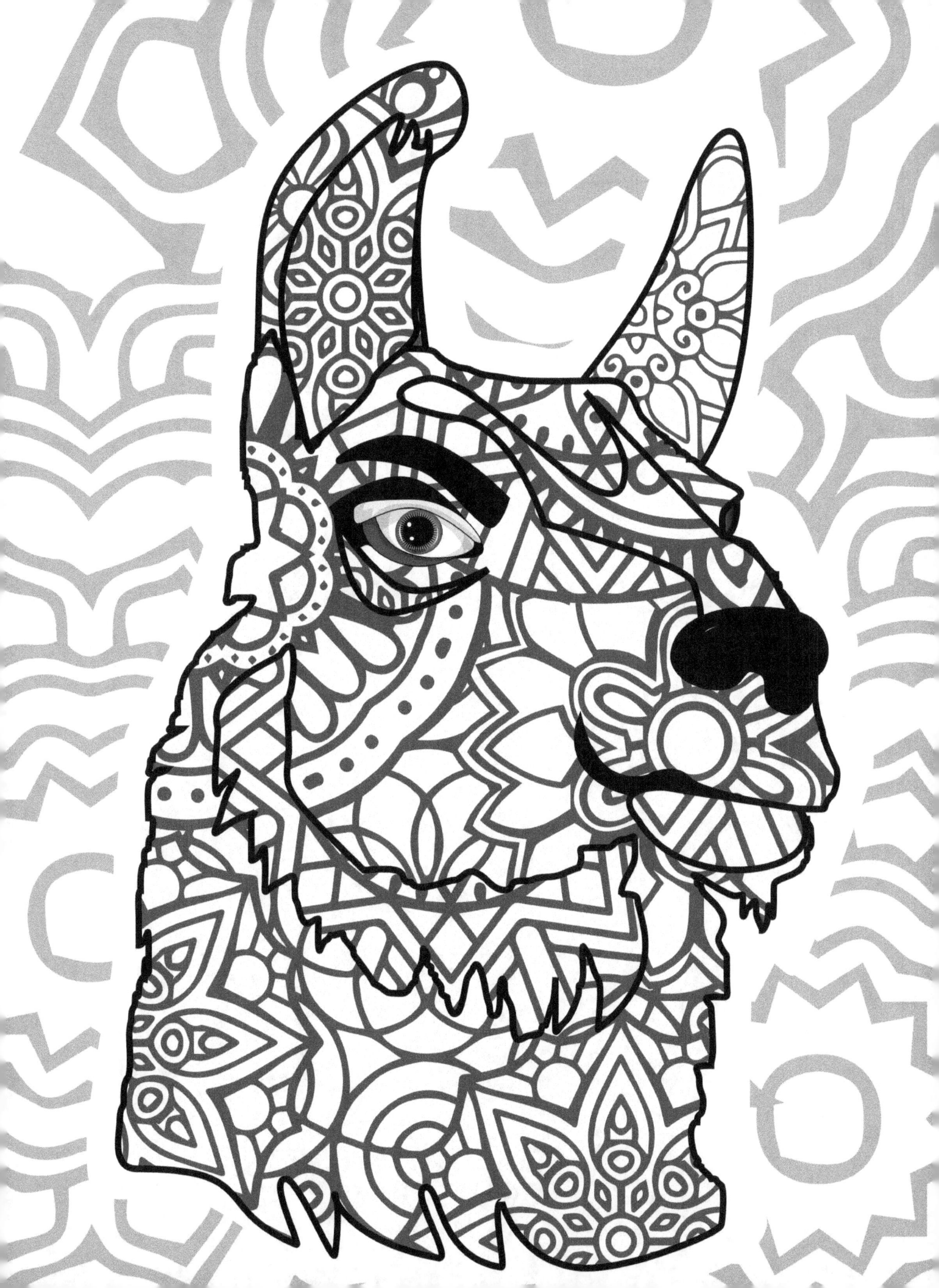

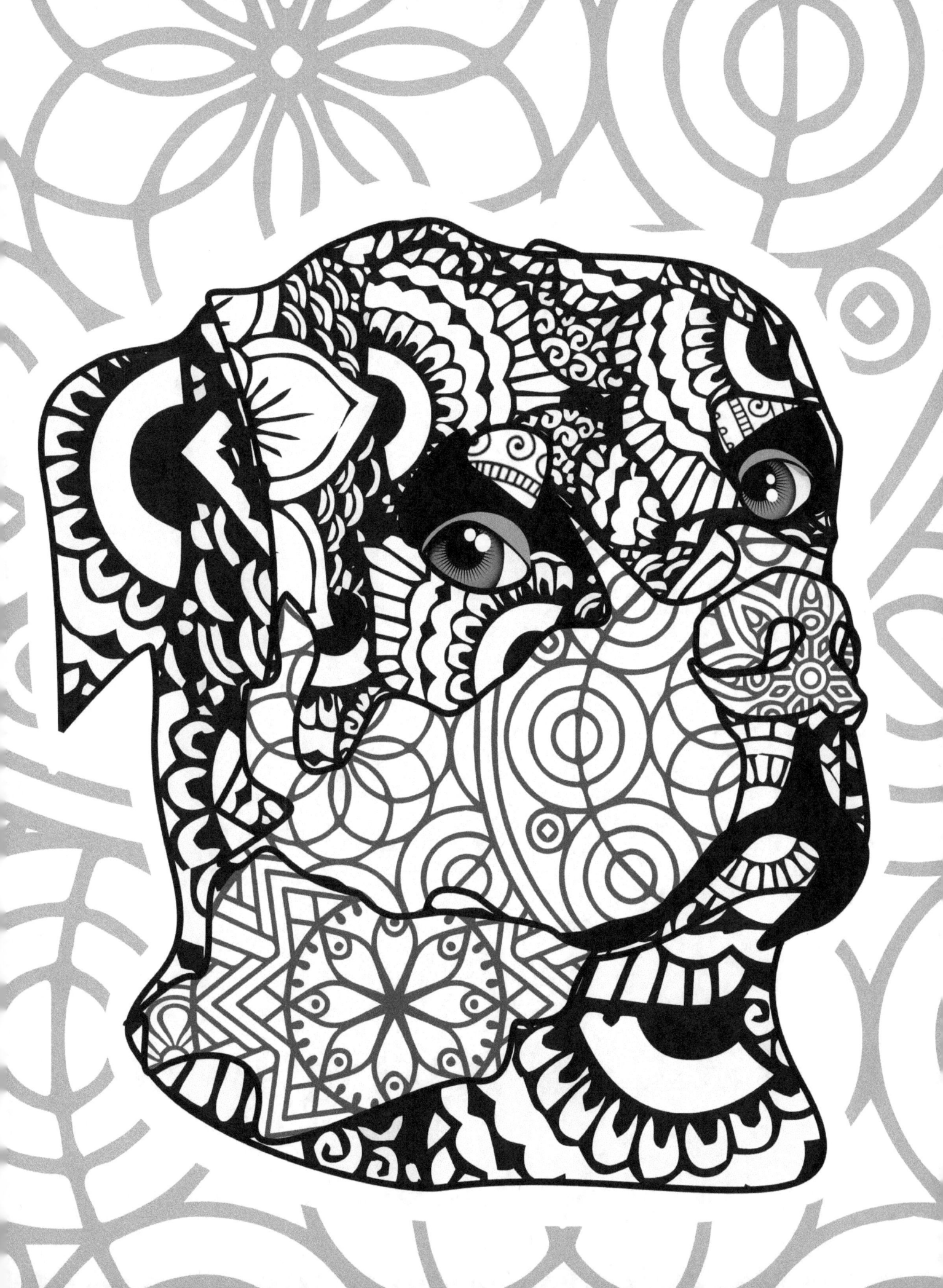

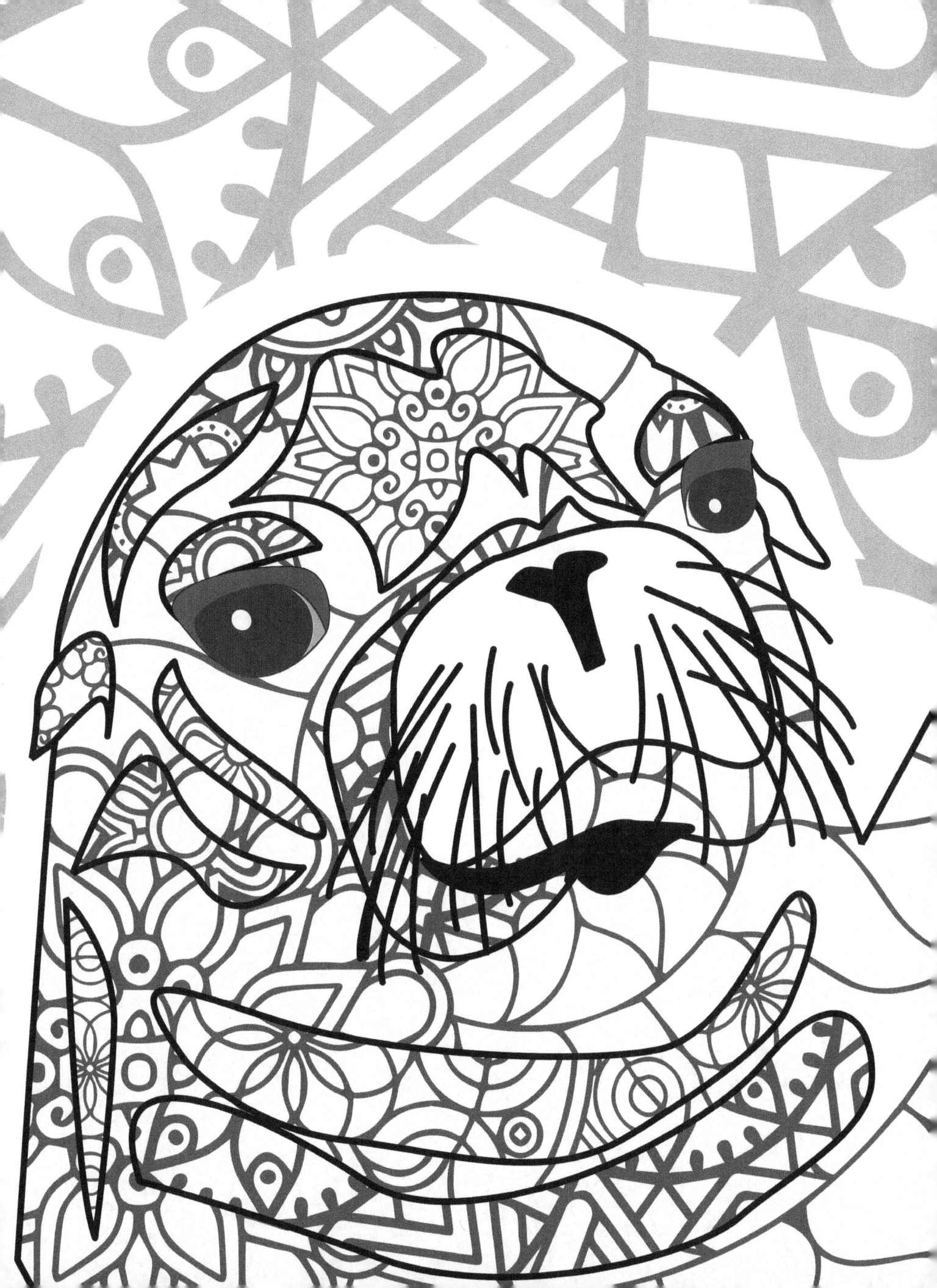

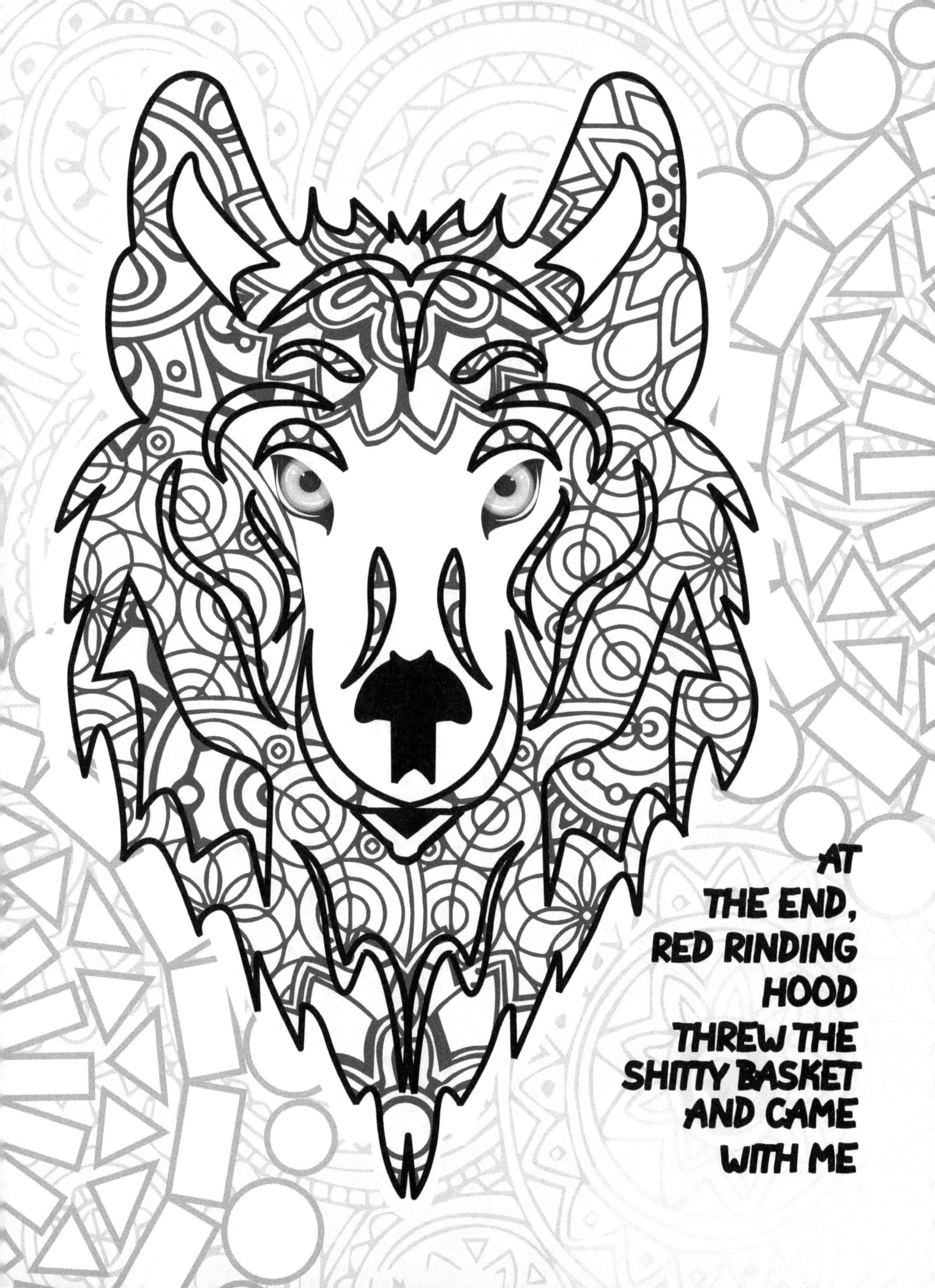

AT THE END, RED RINDING HOOD THREW THE SHITTY BASKET AND CAME WITH ME

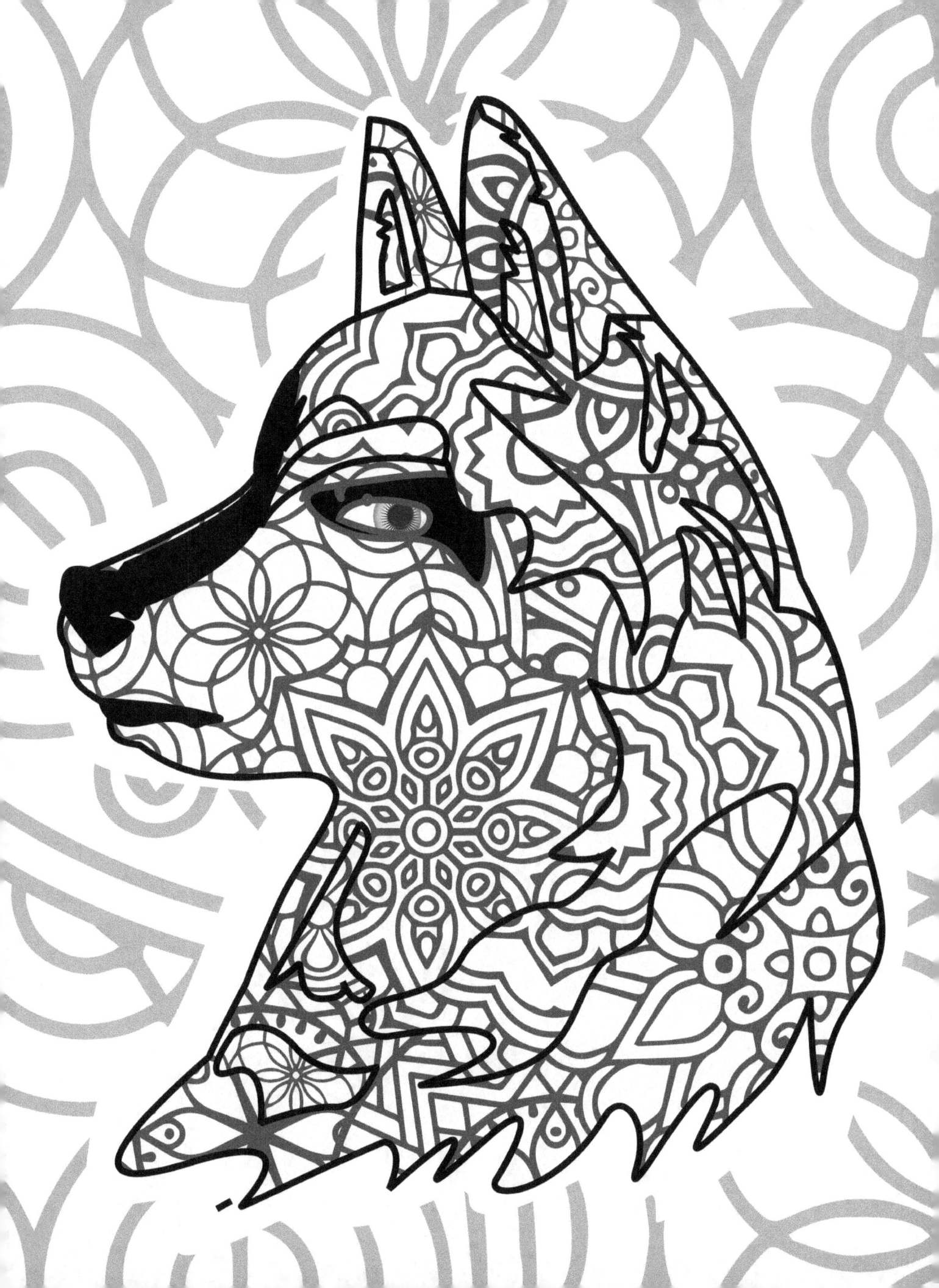

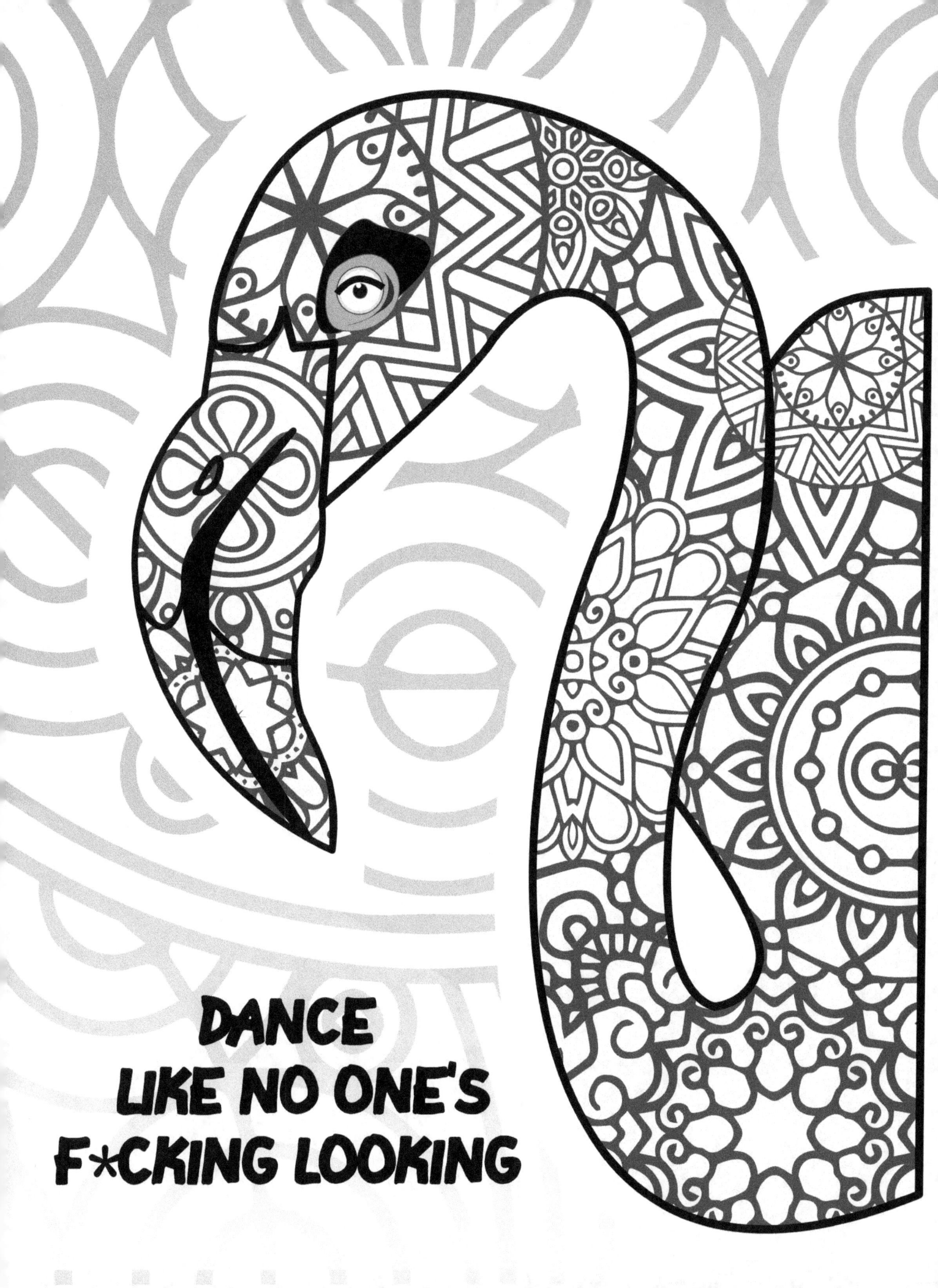

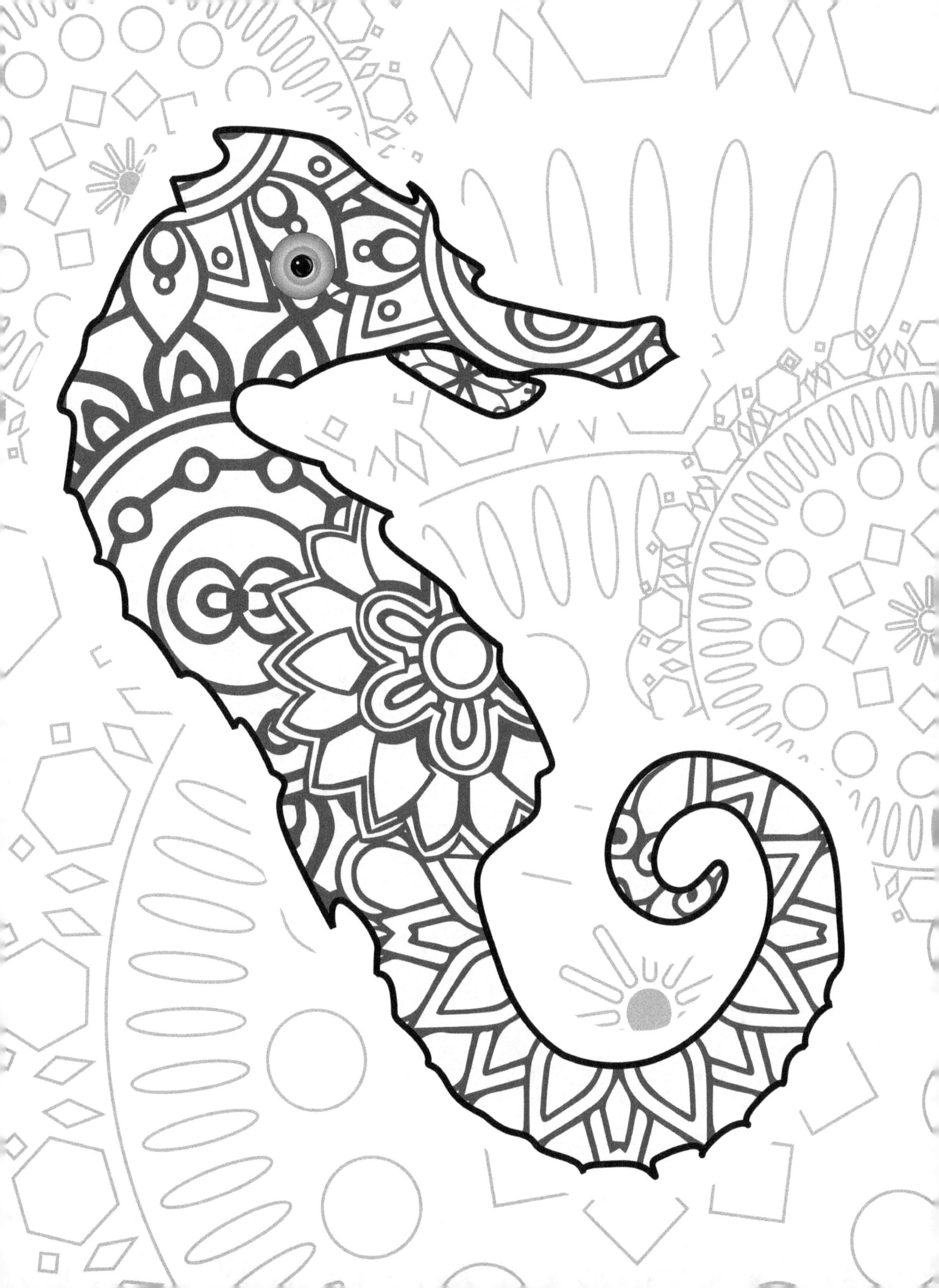

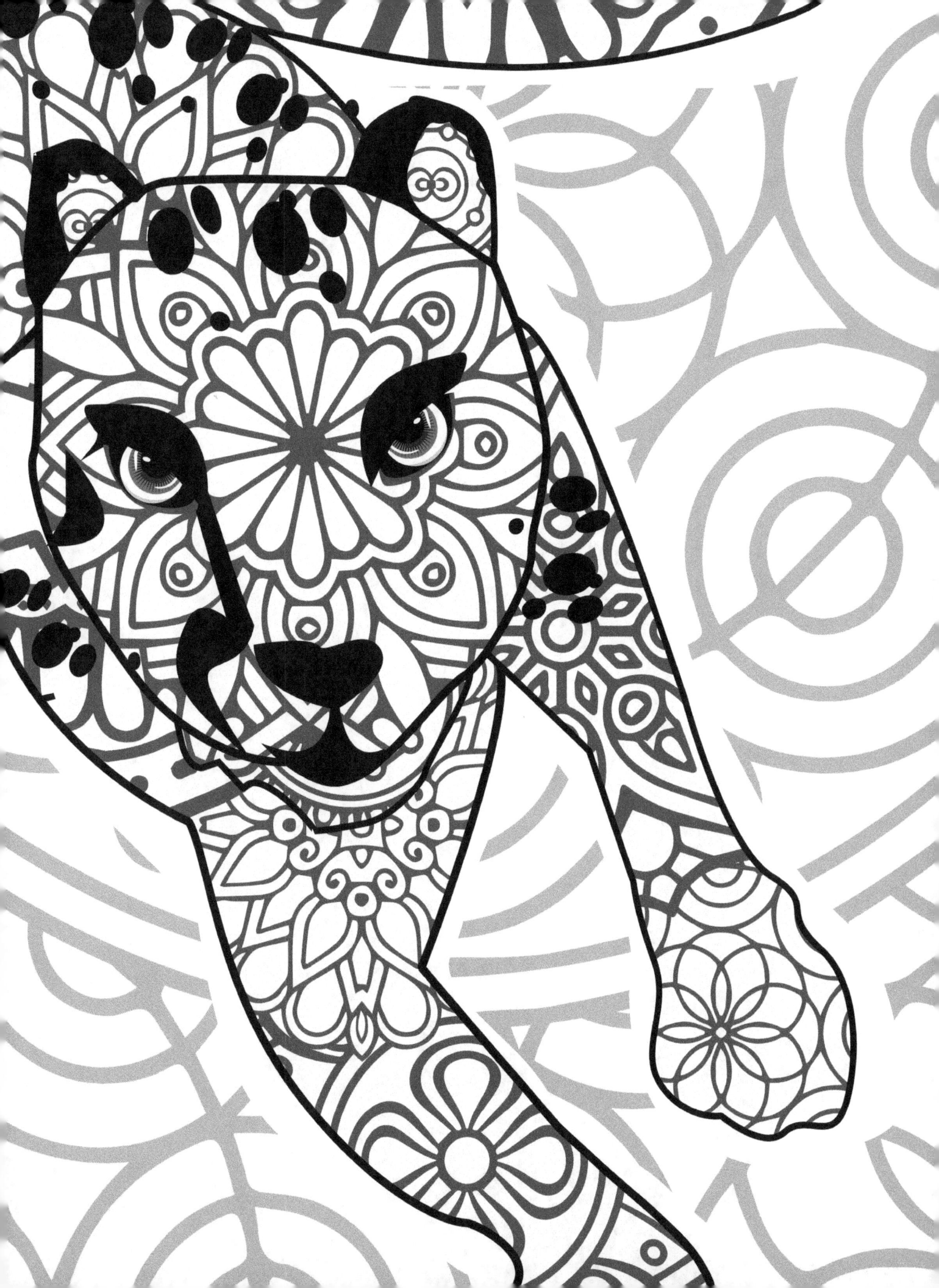

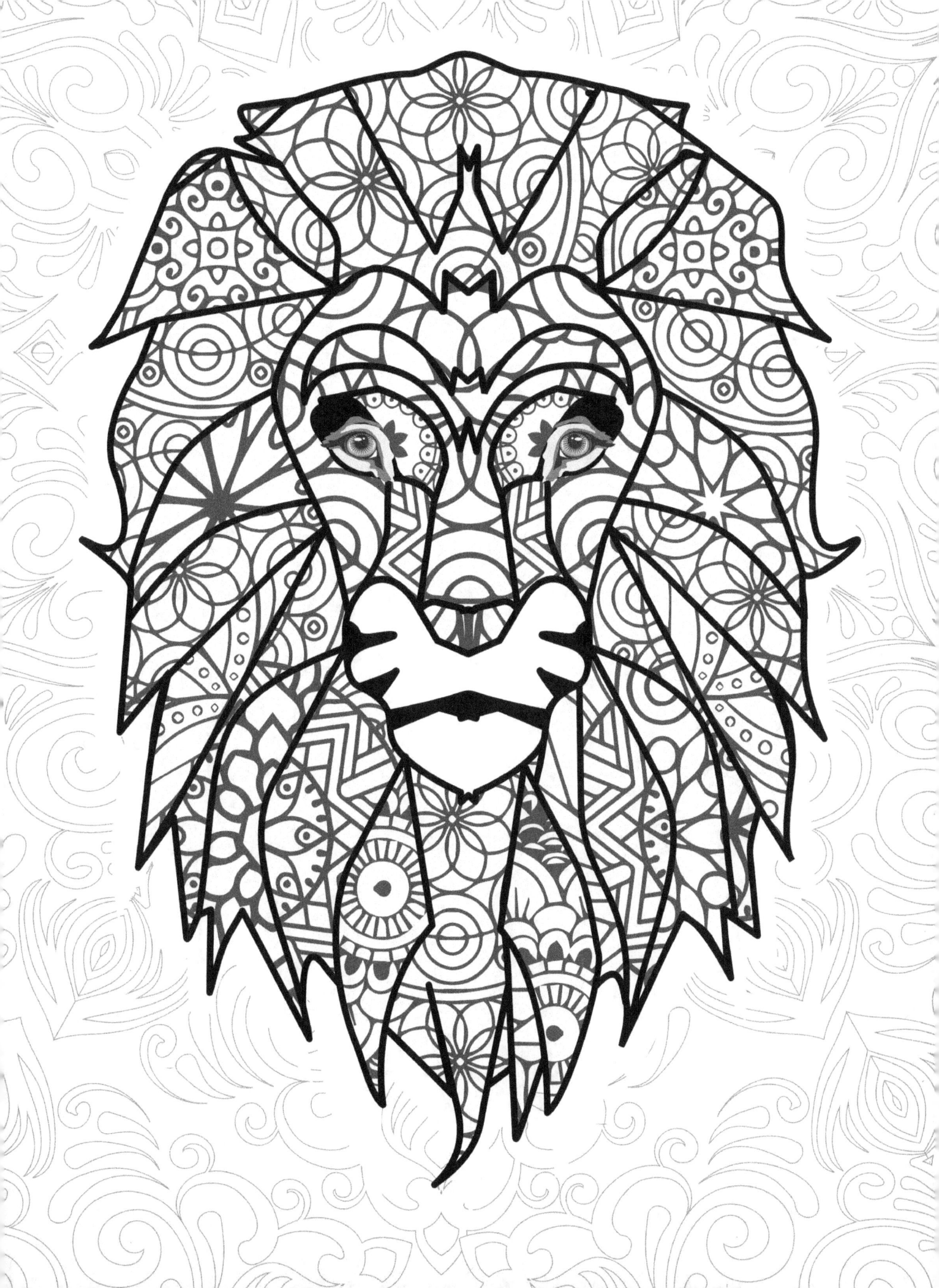

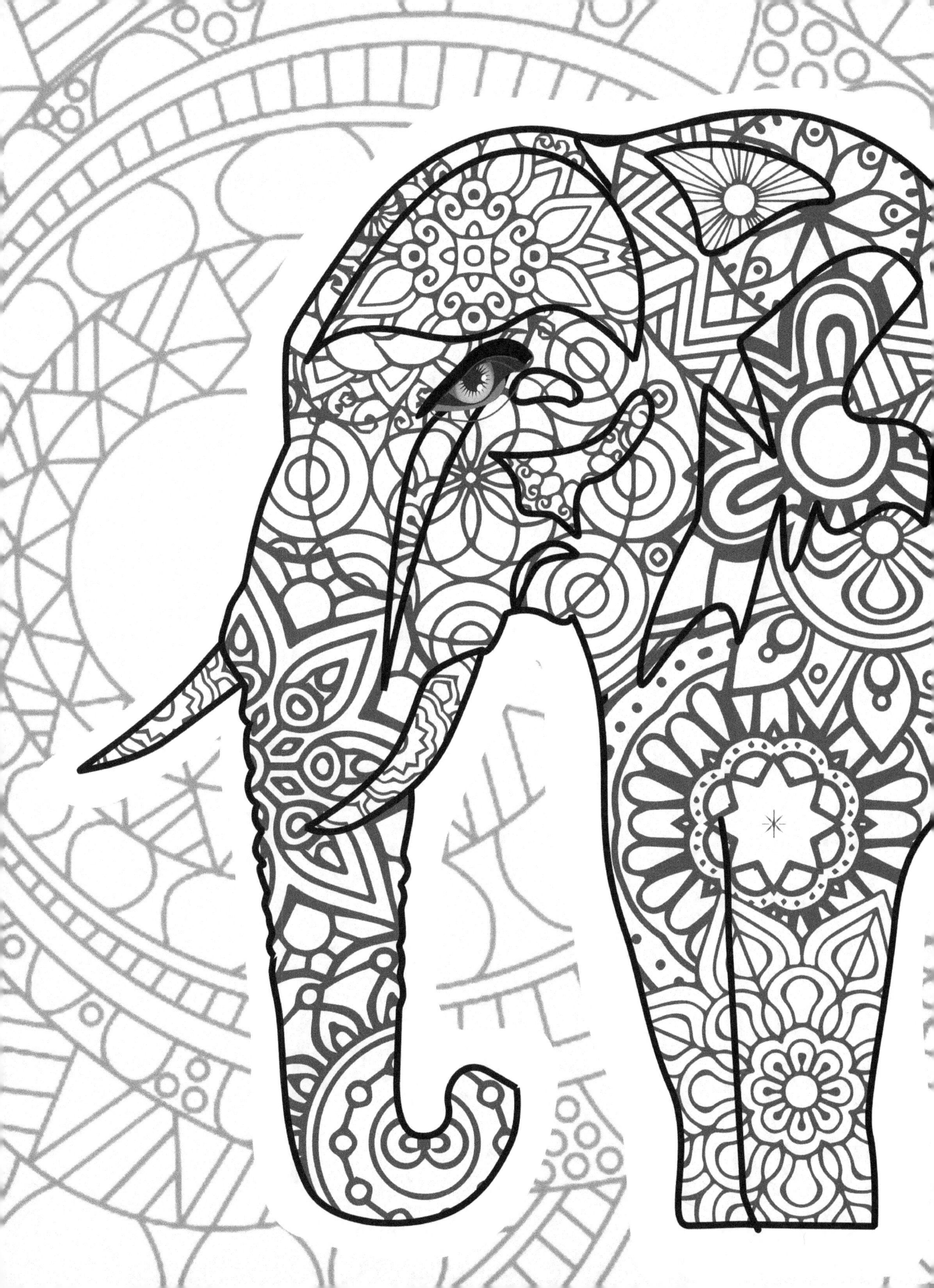

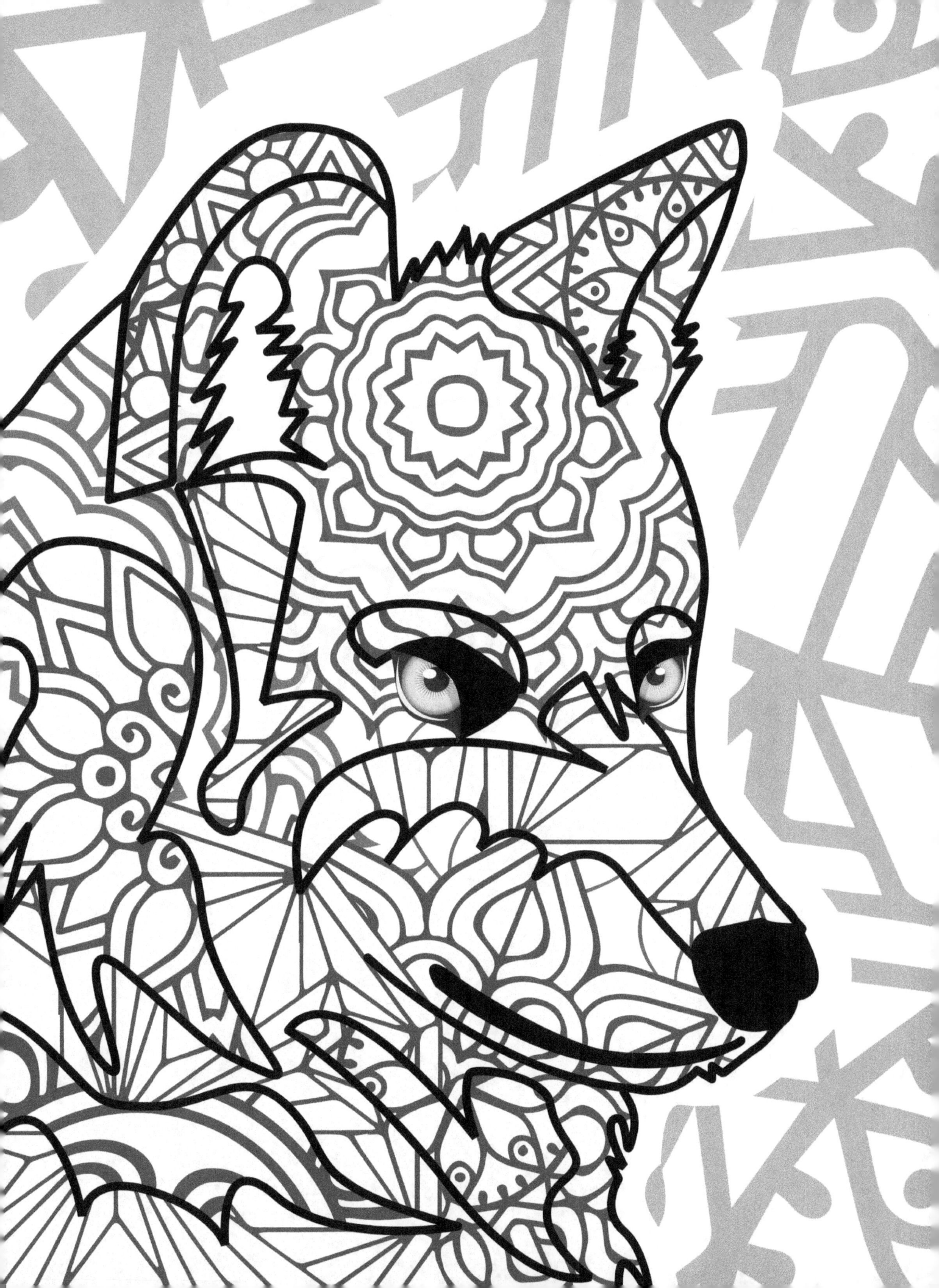

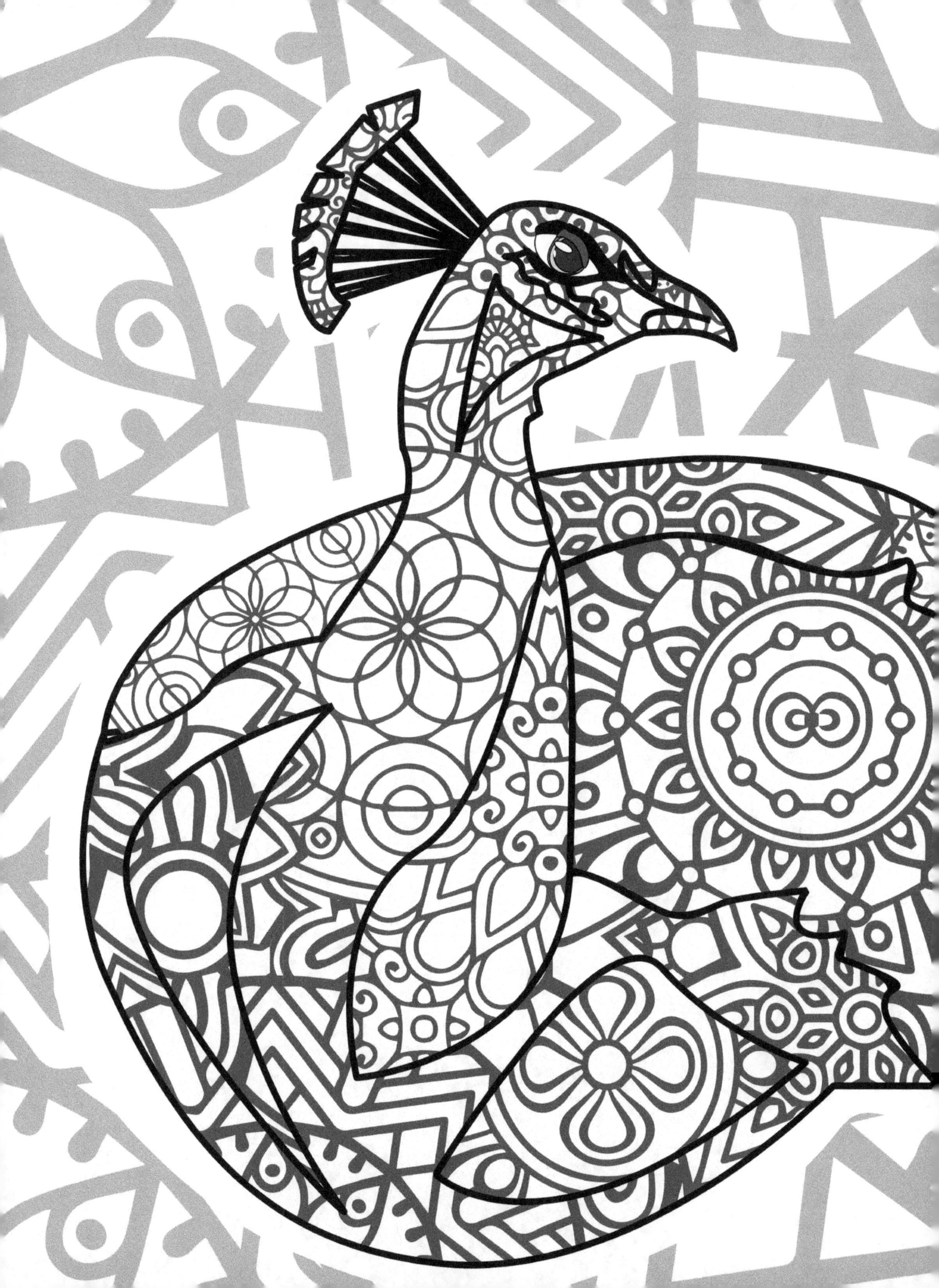

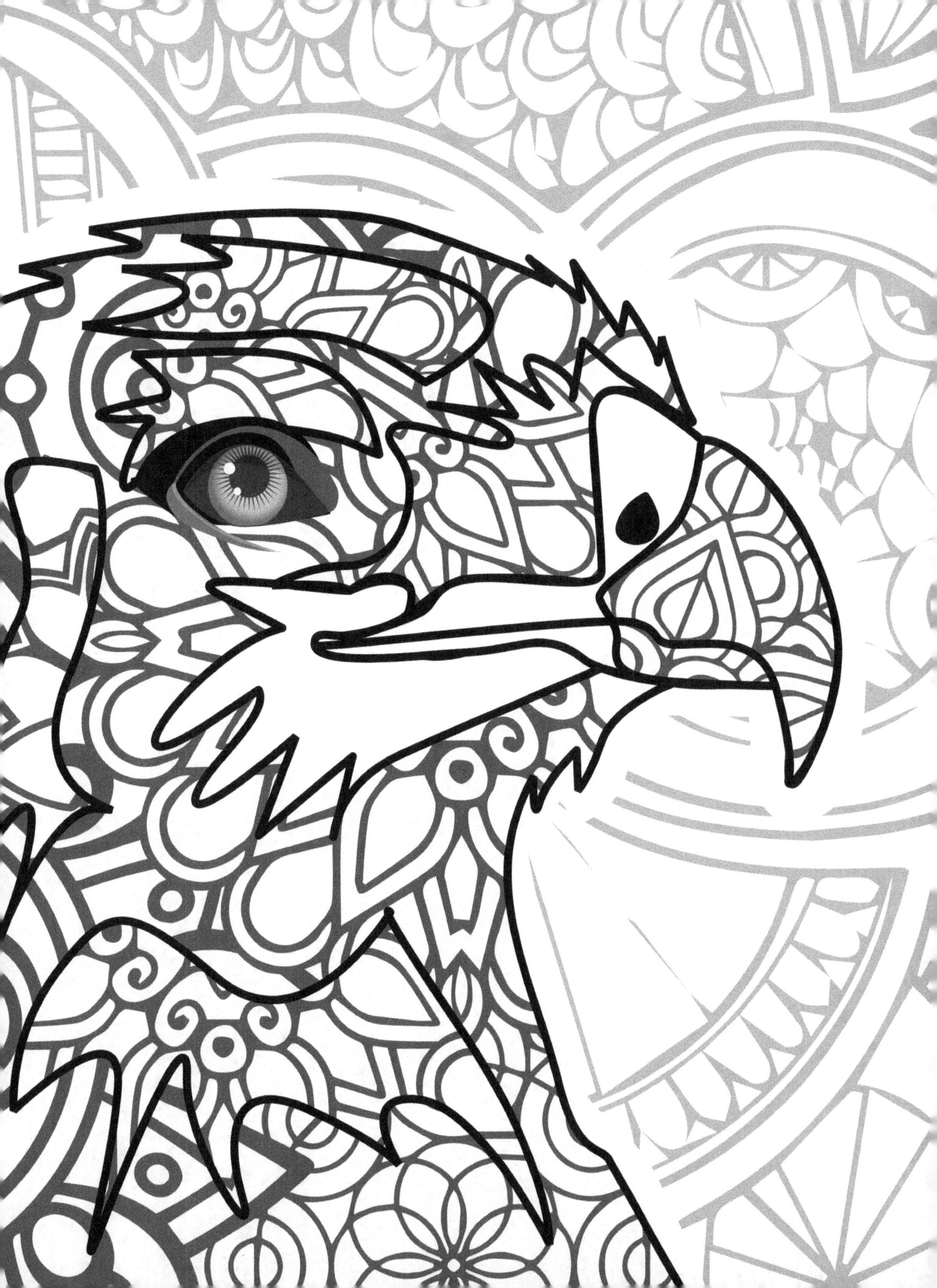

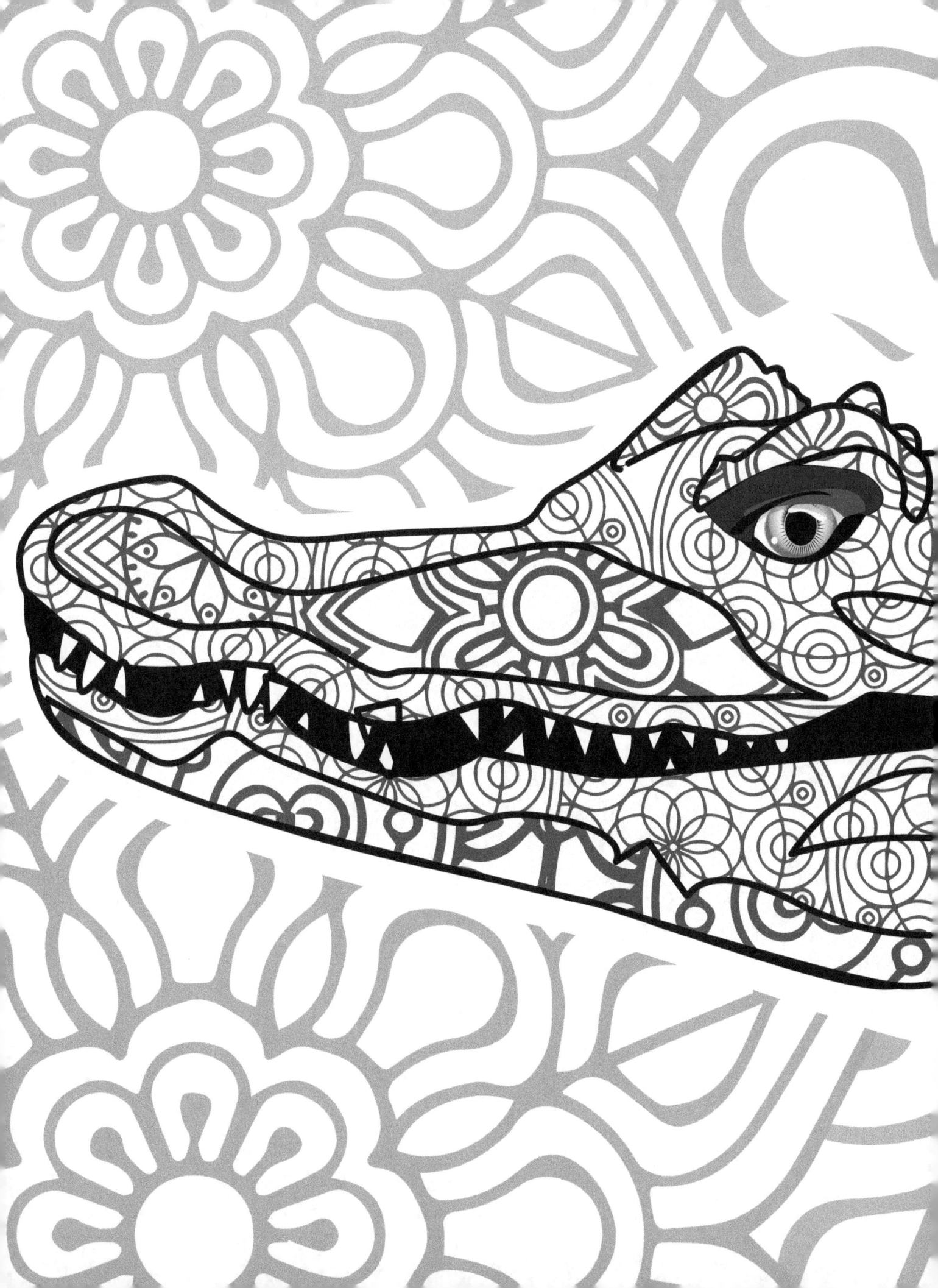

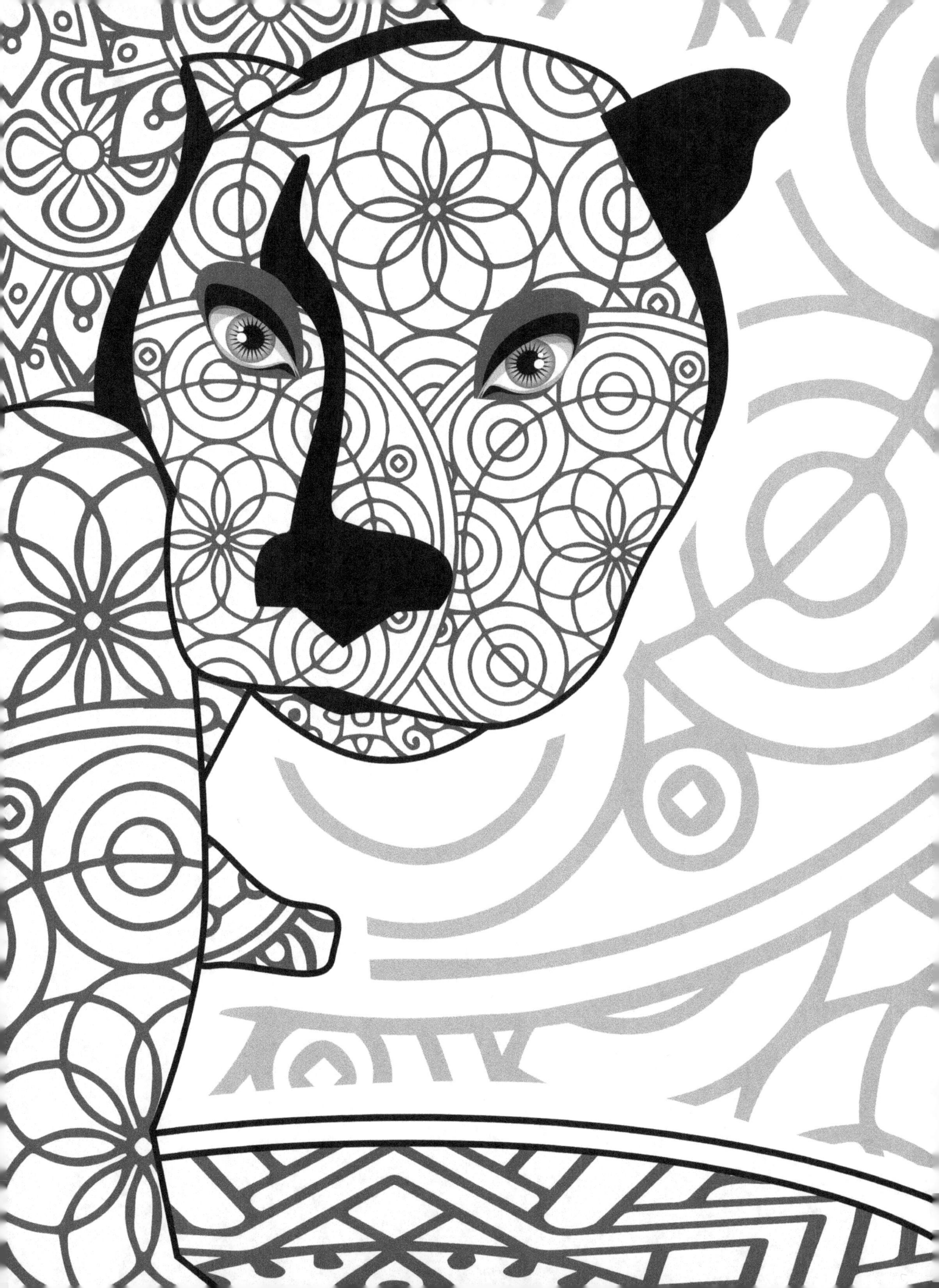

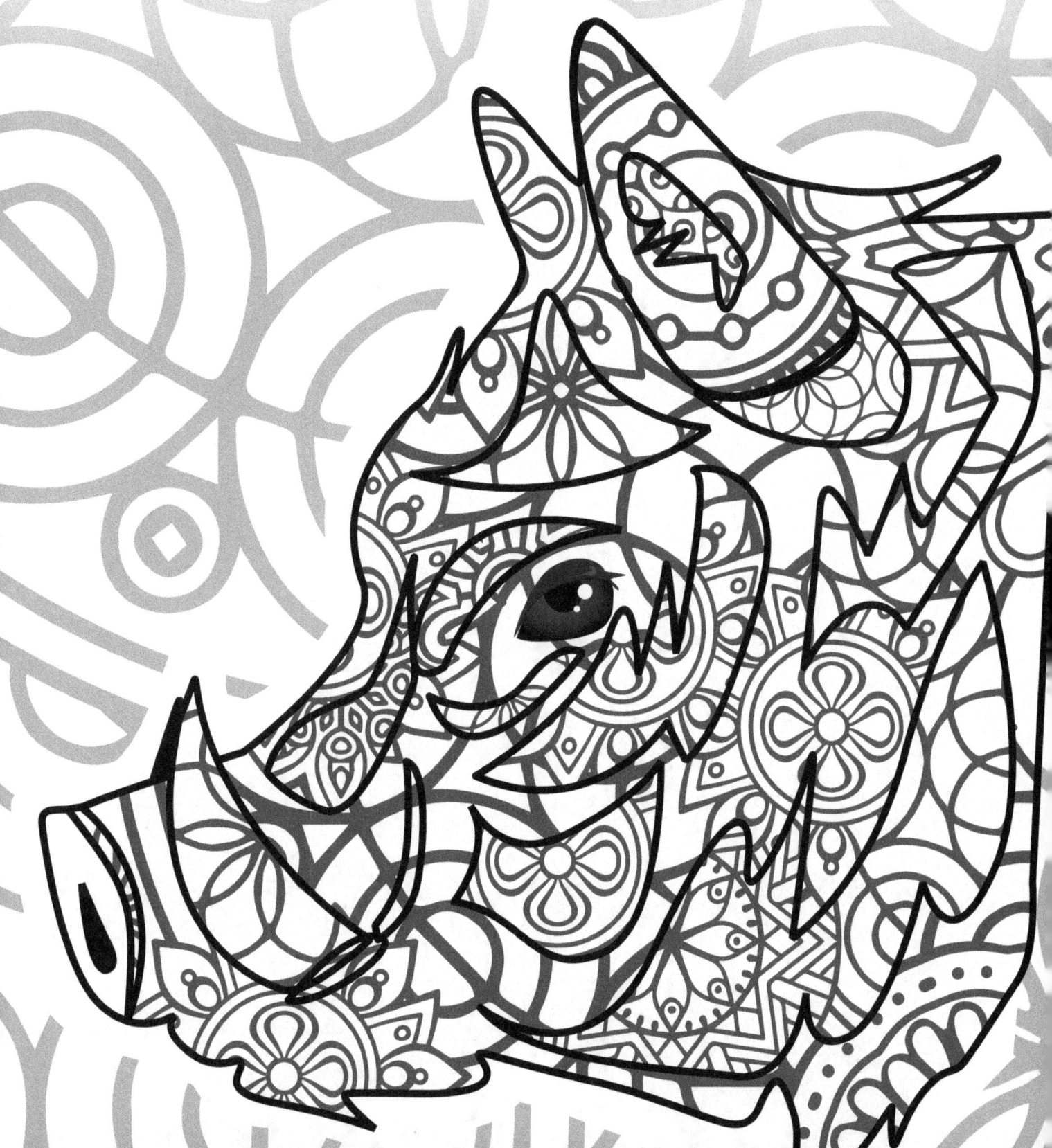

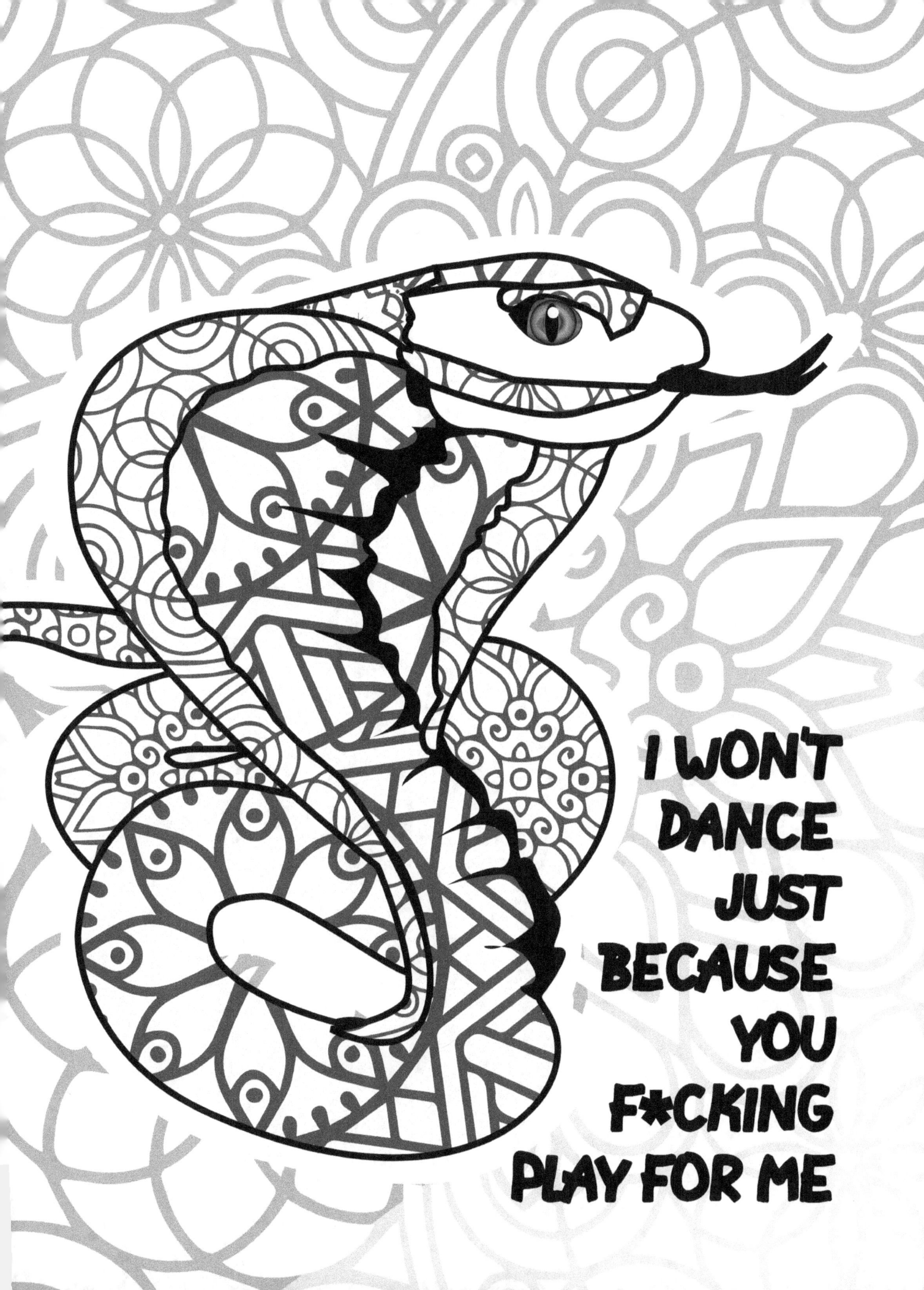

Ready for more?

If you enjoyed this adventure, fasten your seat belts that more are to come! Find me as Emma Russo to keep doing creative Mindfulness in a different way while we enjoy the process.

It would be great if you leave me a review, so many more will benefit from the wisdom of the animal that they carry inside and surrender to the teachings of the Zen masters.

Now that you've had a taste of the benefits of mindfulness, it's not the time to turn back! Keep practicing and free yourself. You will not be able to start a new chapter of your life if you do not close the previous one.

Cheers

Emma R.

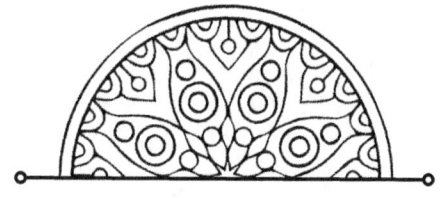